Letts

GCSE Success

Complete Revision & Practice

AQA

Combined Science

Foundation

Exam Practice Workbook

Tom Adams
Dan Evans
Dan Foulder
Dorothy Warren

Biology

Cell Biology

Transport Systems and Photosynthesis

Health, Disease and the Development of Medicines

Coordination and Control

Inheritance, Variation and Evolution

Contents

Contents

1 This image shows some human liver cells, as seen through a very powerful light microscope.

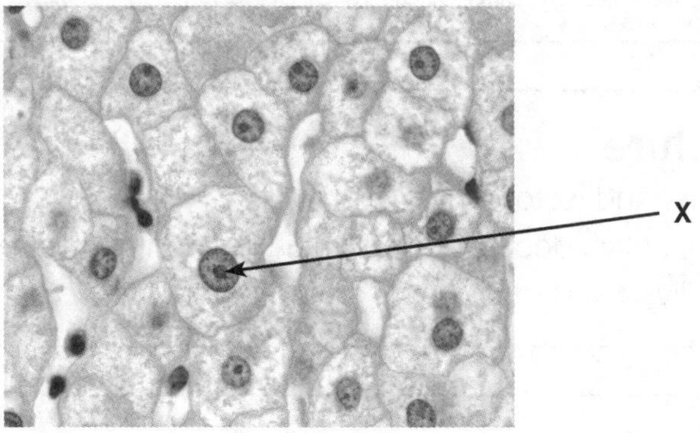

(a) Which organelle is labelled X? nucleus (1)

(b) Unlike skin cells, these cells contain many mitochondria, but they cannot be seen in the image. Suggest why not. (1)

Because it to small.

(c) Why do the cells have many mitochondria? (2)

So it is easier to breath.

(d) Liver cells have different features.
Arrange the features in order of size, starting with the largest. (2)

gene	**nucleus**	**cell**	**chromosome**	**cytoplasm**

2 **(a)** A student is observing bacterial cells under the high power lens of a light microscope. She cannot see a nucleus in the cells and concludes that the cells do not contain DNA. Explain why this conclusion is wrong. (1)

~~All have DNA~~ light microscope only shows 100 nm
~~looking at a prokaryotic cell~~

(b) Which of the following words best describes a bacterial cell? Tick (✓) **one** box. (1)

a Electron microscope could show (1nm)

Prokaryotic	✓
Eukaryotic	
Multicellular	
Undifferentiated	

1 The diagram shows a fertilised egg cell (a zygote).

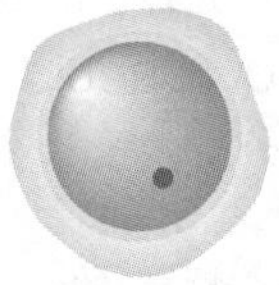

(a) The zygote is described as a **stem cell**. What does this term mean? (1)

They are unSpecified and undifferentiated

(b) The zygote has a very different appearance to the root hair cell (pictured right). However, all cells have some structures in common. Write down **two** of these structures. (2)

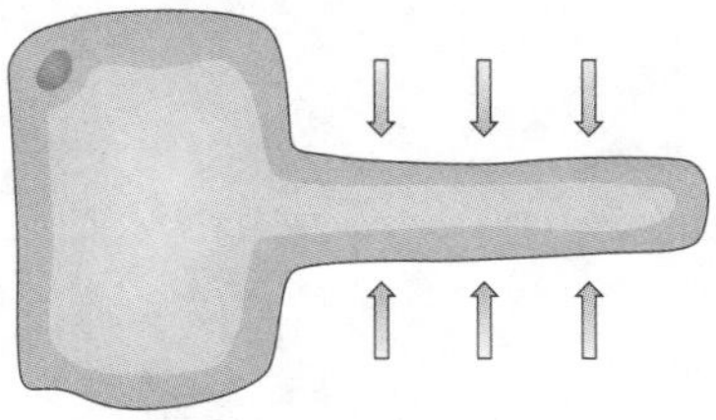

1. cell membrane

2. Nucleus.

2 **(a)** A student attends a school trip to a medical research laboratory, where he is given a talk from a scientist on the techniques and benefits of stem cell research.

Describe **two** applications of stem cell research that the scientist is likely to mention. (2)

1. useful in Studyind how cell division goes wrong

2. in future stem cells could be used to grow new organs for transplants

(b) After the visit, one of the student's friends says she is opposed to stem cell research. Describe **one** objection that people have to stem cell research. (1)

Some people belive embryo at any Stage is human being and Shouldn't be experimented on.

3 A live sperm cell is observed under the microscope beating its tail. It moves across the field of view at a rate of 200 μm every 30 seconds.

Assuming the sperm travels at the same rate and in the same direction, how far will it have travelled in one hour? Give your answer in mm. (3)

24,000μm

1 **(a)** Daljit is looking at some cheek cells using a light microscope under low power. He decides that he wants a more magnified view. How should he adjust the microscope?

Draw a line from X to show which part of the microscope he should adjust. (1)

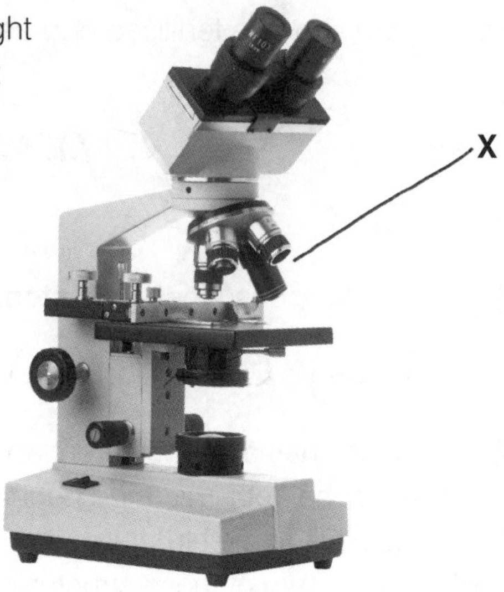

(b) Under higher power, Daljit clearly sees the nucleus, cytoplasm and cell membrane of the cheek cells. He would also like to see mitochondria and ribosomes. Give **two** reasons why he cannot see these structures. (2)

There to small

Using wrong ~~magnif~~ microscope

(c) Using a specially fitted camera, Daljit takes a picture of the cells he sees. He measures the diameter of one cell on his photograph by drawing a line and using a ruler. The line is shown on the picture. It measures 3 cm.

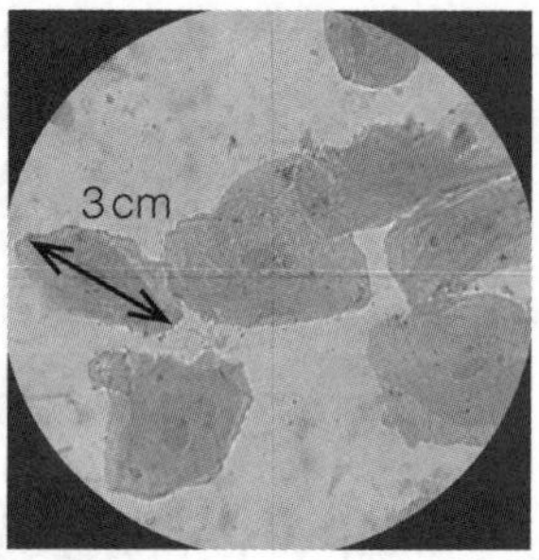

If the microscope magnifies the image 400 times, calculate the actual size of the cell in μm.

You can use the following formula:

$$\text{magnification} = \frac{\text{size of image}}{\text{size of real object}}$$

Answer: 0.0075 μm (3)

2 **(a)** Look at the photograph on the right. What type of microscope was used to take this picture? (1)

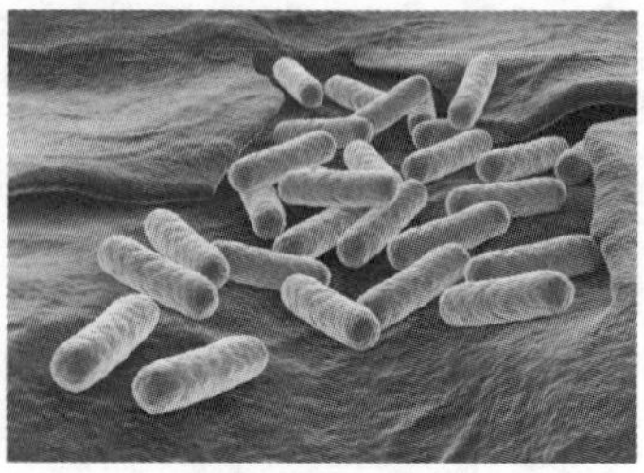

Electron microscope.

(b) There are 27 bacterial cells in this picture. If the bacteria have reproduced from 1 cell every 20 minutes, how long have the bacteria been growing? (2)

520 minutes

1 The illustrations show a single-celled organism, called an amoeba, and a multicellular organism (a horse).

Not to scale

Explain why the horse has specialised organs in its breathing and digestive system, and the amoeba has none. (2)

....

....

....

....

2 Complete the following table, which compares the processes of mitosis and meiosis. (3)

Mitosis	Meiosis
Involved in asexual reproduction	Sexually reproducing
Produces new cells	Produces variation
Produces cells with 46 chromosomes	~~Produces cells~~ 23

3 Jenny is studying chicken cells and is looking at some examples down the microscope. She draws these cells.

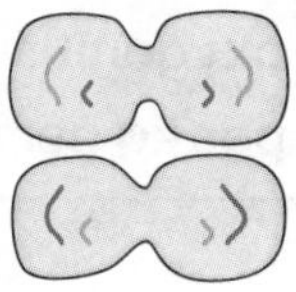

(a) Which type of cell division is shown here? meiosis (1)

(b) Give a reason for your answer to **(a)**. (1)

Shows the 5th step.

4 **(a)** Explain the difference between a **benign** and a **malignant** tumour. (2)

benign don't spread from original esite. malignant spreads to other part of the body.

(b) Write down **two** lifestyle choices a person could make to reduce their chances of developing cancer. (2)

not smoke tobacco products
eat healthy diet.

1 Isaac is running a marathon. Write a balanced word equation for the main type of respiration that will be occurring in his muscles. (2)

gucose + oxyged → Carbon dioxide + water.

2 Isaac's metabolic rate is monitored as part of his training schedule. He is rigged up to a metabolic rate meter. This measures the volumes of gas that he breathes in and out. The difference in these volumes represents oxygen consumption. This can be used in a calculation to show metabolic rate.

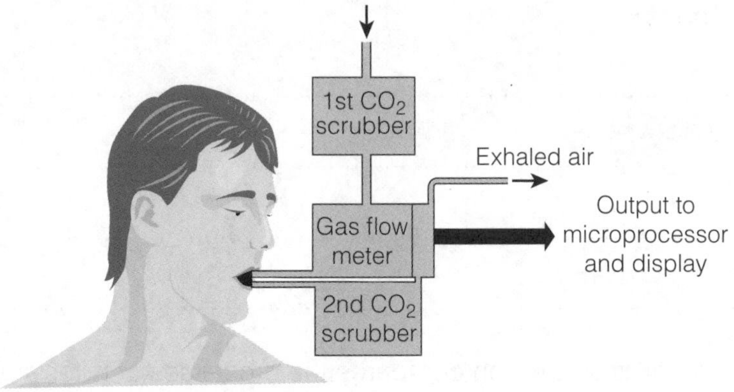

The table below shows some measurements taken from the meter over a period of one hour.

	Five minutes of jogging	Five minutes of rest	Five minutes of sprinting	Five minutes sprinting on an incline
Mean metabolic rate per ml oxygen used per kg per min	35	20	45	60

(a) The units of metabolic rate are expressed in the table as 'per kg'. Why is this adjustment made? (2)

....

....

(b) Using the table, explain the difference in readings for jogging and sprinting. (2)

....

(c) Isaac does quite a lot of exercise. His friend Boris does not. How might Boris' readings compare with Isaac's? Give a reason for your answer. (2)

....

....

1 In an experiment to investigate the enzyme catalase, potato extract was added to a solution of hydrogen peroxide. The catalase in the potato catalysed the decomposition of the hydrogen peroxide and produced oxygen bubbles. The experiment was carried out at different temperatures and the results recorded in the table below.

Temperature / °C	0	10	20	30	40	50	60	70	80
Number of bubbles produced in one minute	0	10	24	40	48	38	8	0	0

(a) Plot a graph of these results on the graph paper. (3)

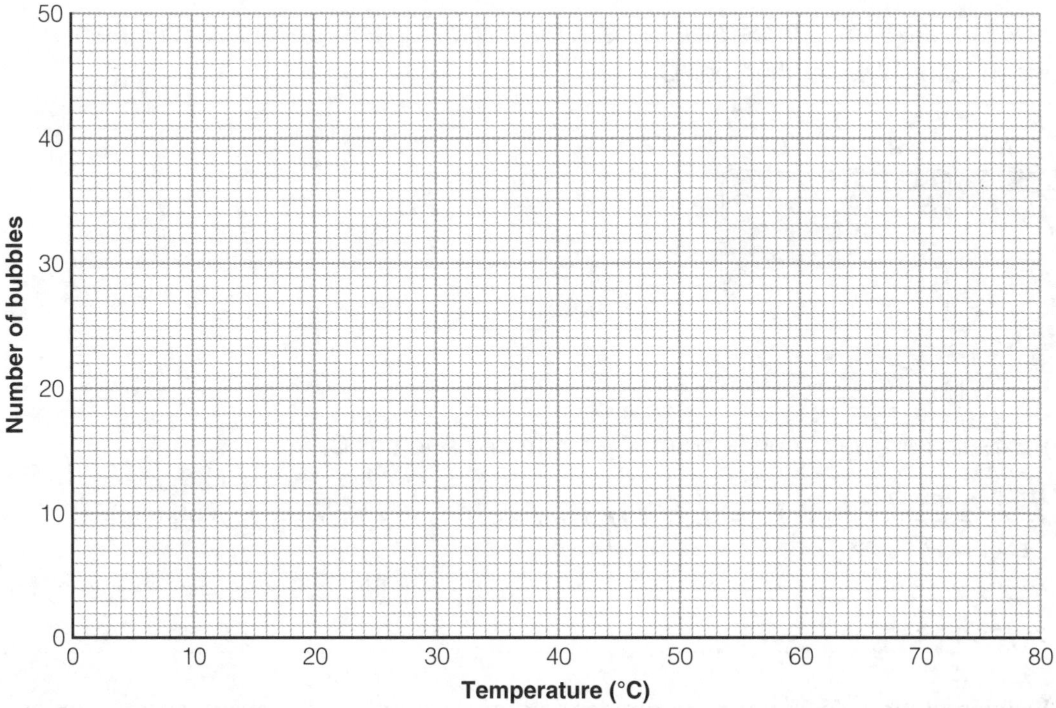

(b) Describe how the number of bubbles produced varies with the temperature of the reacting mixture. (2)

....

....

(c) Using the graph, estimate the optimum temperature for catalase to work at. (1)

....

(d) Factors other than temperature affect the activity of enzymes. Explain why the enzyme amylase, found in saliva, stops working when it gets to the stomach. (2)

....

....

1 Cells rely on diffusion as a way of transporting materials inwards and outwards.

(a) Name **two** substances that move by diffusion **into** animal cells. (2)

~~Carbon dioxide~~ oxygen .... and ~~urea~~ g water ....

(b) Name **one** substance that might diffuse **out** of an animal cell. (1)

Carbon dioxide ....

2 Osmosis is a special case of diffusion involving water. Plants rely on osmosis for movement of materials around their various structures.

Below is a diagram of three plant cells in the root of a plant. Cell **A** has a higher concentration of water than cell **C**.

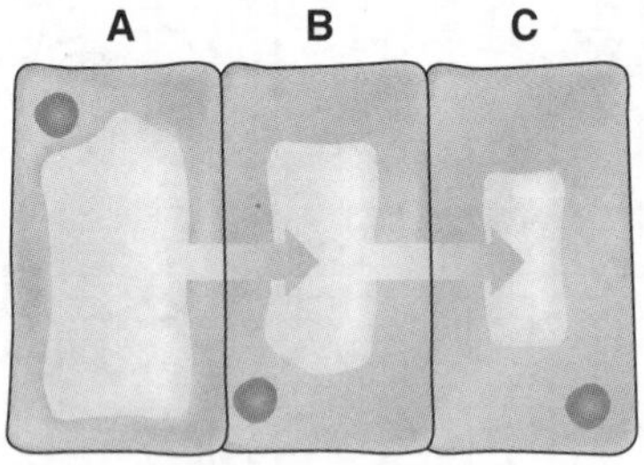

(a) Explain how water can keep moving from cell **A** to cell **C**. (3)

....

....

....

(b) Which of the following are examples of osmosis? Tick (✓) the **three** correct options. (3)

Water evaporating from leaves	☐
Water moving from plant cell to plant cell	✓
Mixing pure water and sugar solution	✓
A pear losing water in a concentrated solution of sugar	☐
Water moving from blood plasma to body cells	✓
Sugar being absorbed from the intestine into the blood	☐

1 This diagram shows a magnified view of the inside of a leaf. Complete the missing labels. (3)

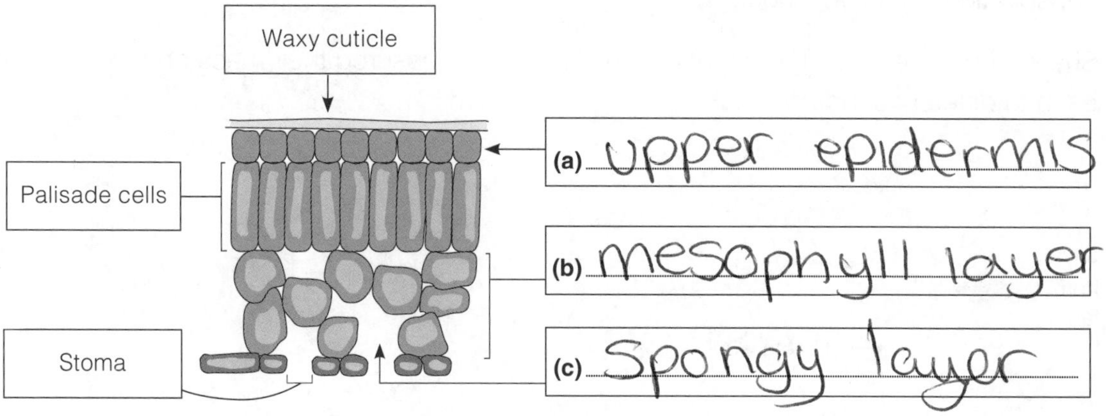

2 Plants all share a basic structure consisting of four main organs.

Describe the function that each organ performs in the plant. (4)

Roots: ....

Stem: ....

Leaf: ....

Flower: ....

3 Describe **three** adaptations of xylem vessels that make them suited to the job they do. (3)

....

....

4 The diagram shows xylem and phloem tissue.

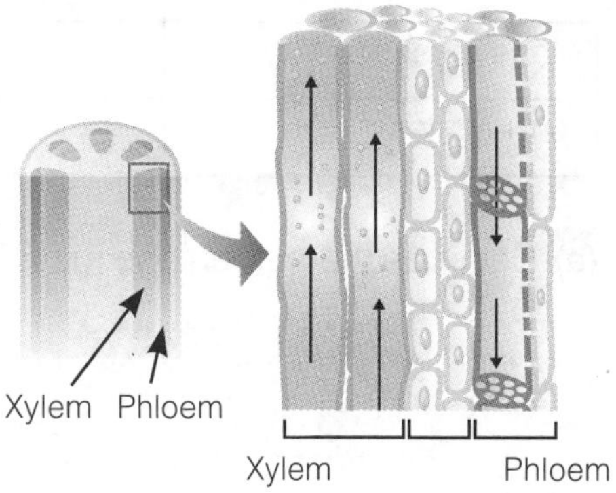

(a) State **one** structural difference between the two tissues. (1)

....

....

(b) Small, herbivorous insects called aphids are found on plant stems. They have piercing mouthparts that can penetrate down to the phloem.

Explain the reasons for this behaviour. (2)

....

....

1 In an experiment, a plant biologist carried out an investigation to measure the rate of transpiration in a privet shoot.

She set up three tubes like the one in the diagram, measured their mass and exposed them each to different conditions.

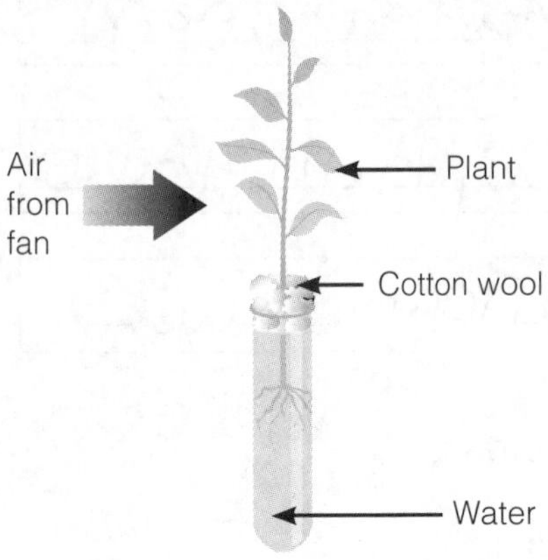

- **A** – Left to stand in a rack
- **B** – Cold moving air from a fan was blown over it
- **C** – A radiant heater was placed next to it

The tubes were left for six hours and then their masses were re-measured.

The biologist recorded the masses in this table.

Tube	A	B	C
Mass at start (g)	41	43	45
Mass after six hours (g)	39	35	37
Mass loss (g)	2	8	5
% mass loss	4.9		11.9

(a) Calculate the percentage mass loss in tube B. Show your working. (2)

....

....

(b) Which factor increased the rate of transpiration the most? .... (1)

(c) Evaporation from the leaves has increased in tubes B and C. Describe how this would affect water in the xylem vessels of the plant. (1)

....

1 The graph shows the number of people who die from coronary heart disease per 100 000 people in different parts of the UK.

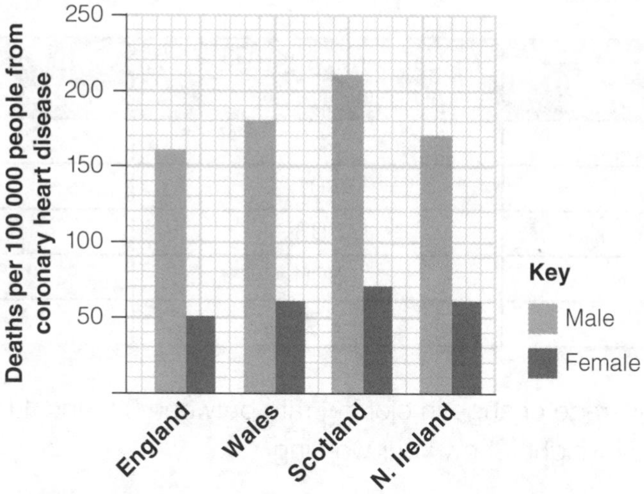

(a) (i) Which country has the highest number of deaths per 100 000? (1)

Scotland

(ii) Calculate the difference between this country's death rate for males and the country with the smallest death rate for males. (1)

....

(b) Describe the pattern between death rates from coronary heart disease in men and women. (1)

Women are lower then men

2 The diagram shows the human circulatory system.

Match the numbers on the diagram with the words listed below. Write the appropriate numbers in the boxes. (4)

Artery	3
Capillaries in the body	4
Vein	1
Capillaries in the lungs	2

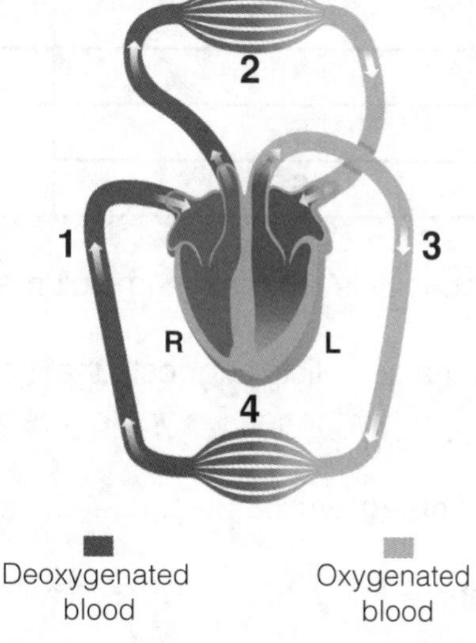

Transport in humans 1

Module 10

1 The table shows some data from an experiment measuring the effect of different doses of warfarin in two samples of rat blood. Warfarin prevents blood from clotting, killing the rat as a result of internal bleeding.

Warfarin dose / mg per kg body weight	Time for clot to form in sample 1	Time for clot to form in sample 2
0.2	52	61
0.4	101	99
0.6	193	197
0.8	300	311
1	978	984

(a) Calculate the average change in clotting rate between 0.2 and 1.0 mg of warfarin per kilogram of body weight. Show your working. (2)

....

....

(b) Explain why the warfarin dose was measured in mg per kg of body weight. (1)

....

(c) Describe the pattern of results shown in the data. (1)

....

2 Scientists are studying the performance of pearl divers living on a Japanese island. They have timed how long they can stay underwater. The scientists have also measured recovery time for the divers' breathing rates after a dive. The data is shown in the table below.

Vital capacity / litres	Max. time under water / mins
3.5	2.5
4.0	2.7
4.3	2.8
4.5	2.9
4.6	3.0

Vital capacity is the maximum volume of air that the lungs can hold at any one time.

One of the scientists suggests that having a larger vital capacity allows a diver to stay underwater for longer. Do you agree with her? Give a reason for your answer. (2)

Agree / disagree: ....

Reason: ....

....

1. A group of students undertook a common experiment to prove that leaves carry out photosynthesis. They selected one plant from their classroom windowsill and covered part of a single leaf in foil. The students then carried out experiments testing for the presence of starch using iodine (a yellow brown liquid). A positive starch test will turn iodine blue / black.

(a) What is prevented from reaching the leaf by the foil? Sunlight (1)

(b) If the leaf covered in foil was tested for starch using iodine solution, what result would you expect? (1)

....

(c) One student suggests that they should make their result more reliable. What should they do? (1)

Test them again.

(d) Another student in the class says that they should have a control in their investigation. What would they use as the control? (1)

....

2. Glucose can be used by plants for energy or to build up bigger molecules.
The diagram shows a starch molecule. The part labelled **A** is a glucose molecule.

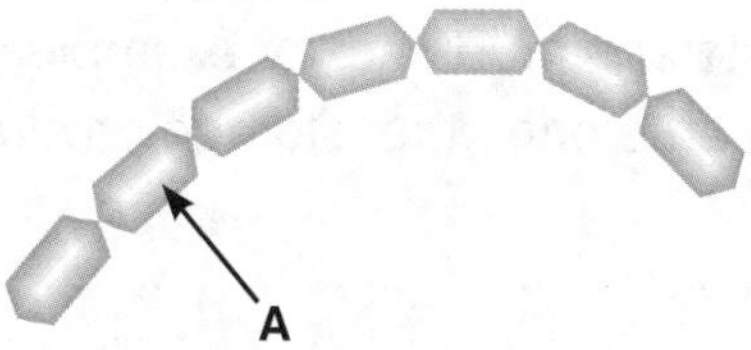

(a) In which organs of the plant would most of this starch be manufactured? (1)

....

(b) The plant can synthesise other molecules from the glucose it manufactures, such as cellulose and protein. State **one** use for each of these molecules. (2)

Cellulose: needed for cell walls.

Protein: Growth and repair of plant tissue

3. **(a)** State the purpose of chlorophyll in photosynthesis. (1)

to absorb Sunlight.

(b) This sketch graph shows the effect of increasing light intensity on the rate of photosynthesis. In region 2, light is no longer acting as a limiting factor.

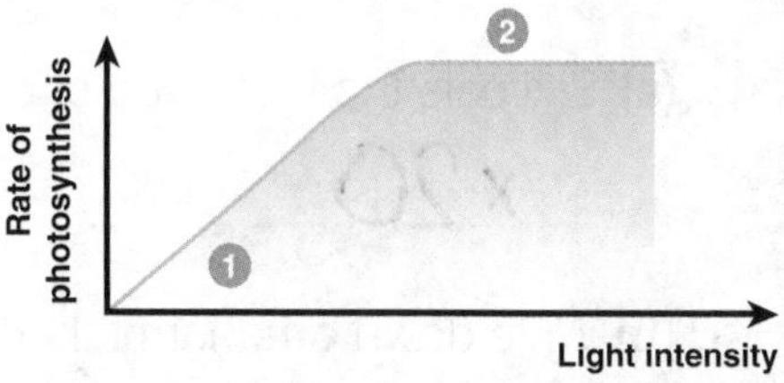

Explain what is meant by **limiting factor** and give **one** example other than light intensity. (2)

will influence the rate of reaction most. Carbon dioxide concentration

1 Obesity is a non-communicable condition. The table shows how obesity in a population of children aged between two and ten changed between 2005–2013.

Year	% of obese children
2005	9.9
2006	10.2
2007	10.8
2008	11.3
2009	11.8
2010	12.3
2011	12.8
2012	13.3
2013	13.7

(a) Predict the percentage of obese children in the UK for 2014 based on this trend. (1)

14.3 %

(b) If the body's daily energy requirements are exceeded, sugar can be converted to storage products; for example, fat under the skin.
Name **one** other storage product and where it would be found. (2)

....

(c) Write down **two** other conditions / diseases that are non-communicable. (2)

....

....

2 The table shows how smoking can affect a person's chances of getting lung cancer.

Number of cigarettes smoked per day	Increased chance of lung cancer compared to non-smokers
5	×4
10	×8
15	×12
20	×16

(a) Estimate the increased chance of lung cancer if someone smoked 25 cigarettes a day. (1)

x20

(b) Write down **one** harmful effect that smoking can have on unborn babies. (1)

Lower birth weight

....

1 Microorganisms consist of bacteria, viruses and protists. Many cause harm to the human body.

(a) Write down the term that describes these disease-causing organisms. (1)

....

(b) Harmful microorganisms produce symptoms when they reproduce in large numbers.

Write down **two** ways in which microorganisms cause these symptoms. (2)

1. ....

2. ....

2 Malaria kills many thousands of people every year. The disease is common in areas that have warm temperatures and stagnant water.

(a) Explain why this is. (2)

....

....

(b) A protist called *Plasmodium* lives in the salivary glands of the female *Anopheles* mosquito.

From the box below, choose a word that describes each organism. (2)

parasite	**disease**	**symptom**
vector	**consumer**	**host**

Mosquito: ....

Plasmodium: ....

(c) Samit, an African villager, believes that having mosquito nets around the beds of family members and taking antiviral remedies will reduce their risk of catching malaria.

Explain why he is only partially correct. (2)

....

....

Communicable diseases

Module 14

1 The diagram shows a white blood cell producing small proteins as part of the body's immune system.

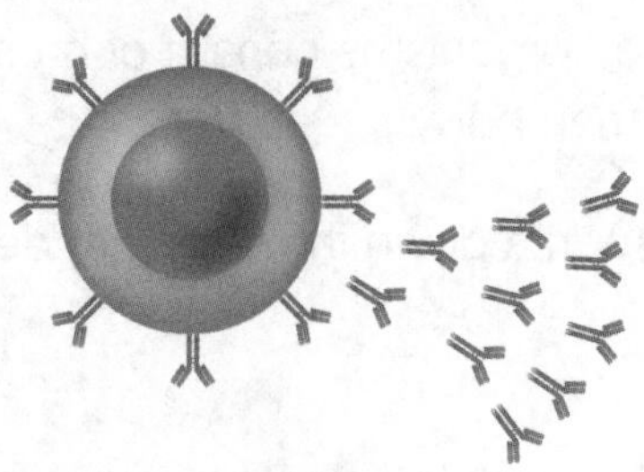

(a) What is the name of these proteins? (1)

....

(b) These proteins will eventually lock on to specific invading pathogens. Describe what happens next to disable the pathogens. (1)

....

....

(c) Below are the names of some defence mechanisms that the body uses. Match each defence mechanism with the correct function. The first one has been done for you. (3)

Epithelial cells in respiratory passages	engulf pathogens.
Phagocytes	contain enzymes called lysozymes that break down pathogen cells.
Tears	contains acid to break down pathogen cells.
Stomach	trap pathogens in mucus.

2 The graph shows the antibody levels in Dominic after he contracted the flu. The flu pathogen first entered his body two days before point X. There was then a second invasion at point Y.

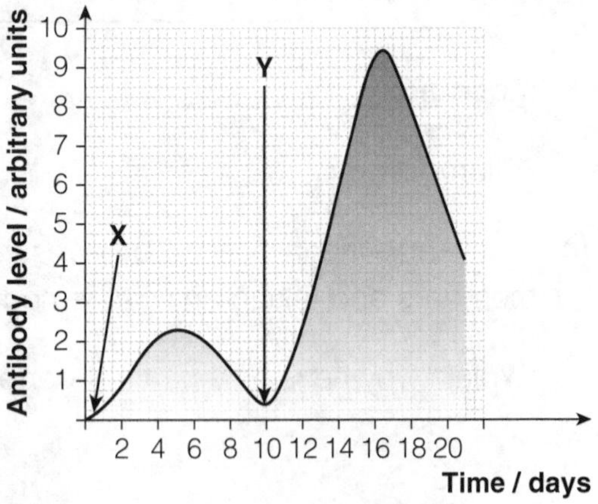

(a) Name **one** transmission method by which Dominic could have caught the flu virus. (1)

....

(b) After how many days did the antibodies reach their maximum level? (1)

.... days

(c) What is the difference in antibody level between point Y and this maximum? Show your working. (2)

.... arbitrary units

(d) Explain, using your knowledge of memory cells, the difference between these two levels. (2)

....

....

1 The MMR vaccine immunises children against measles, mumps and rubella.

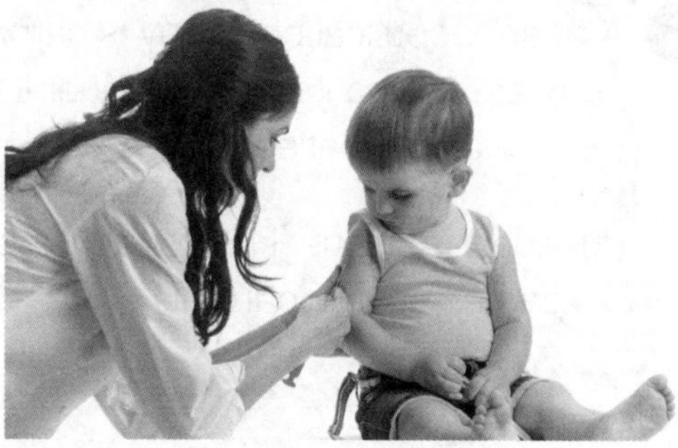

Use your knowledge of the body's immune system and memory cells to explain how antibodies against these diseases are produced. (6)

....

....

....

....

....

....

....

....

....

....

....

....

2 Explain why antibiotics are becoming increasingly less effective against 'superbugs' such as MRSA. (3)

....

....

....

....

Module 17 Discovery and development of drugs

1 A pharmaceutical company is carrying out a clinical trial on a new drug called alketronol. They are testing it to see whether it produces significant adverse (harmful) events in a sample of 226 patients.

(a) Apart from checking for adverse events, write down **two** other reasons that a company carries out clinical trials. (2)

1. ....

2. ....

(b) The kind of trial carried out is a double blind trial. What does this term mean? (2)

....

....

....

(c) Data from the trial is shown in the table below.

Adverse event	Alketronol	Placebo
	Number of patients	**Number of patients**
Pain	4	3
Cardiovascular	21	20
Dyspepsia	7	6
Rash	10	1

(i) Calculate the percentage of patients **in the trial** who suffered a cardiovascular event while taking alketronol. Show your working. (2)

.... %

(ii) A scientist is worried that alketronol may trigger heart attacks. Is there evidence in the data to support this view? Explain your answer. (2)

....

....

....

(iii) Which other adverse event might cause concern? Give a reason for your decision. (2)

....

....

1 From the box below, choose three words to complete the information about how conditions are kept stable in the human body. (3)

effectors	**spine**	**receptors**
homeostasis	**hormones**	**glands**

Certain factors have to be kept constant in the body. This is achieved by a process called .... In order for this to happen, the central nervous system (CNS) needs to receive information from the environment. This is accomplished through .... such as light-sensitive cells on the retina. Once the information has been relayed, the CNS brings about appropriate changes through ....

2 A company is developing technology that allows robots to make decisions in a form of artificial intelligence.

As part of their research, the company tries to model the human nervous system.

(a) Write down the name given to the part of the nervous system that processes information from the senses.

.... (1)

(b) Describe the other parts of the human nervous system that would need to be reproduced so that the robots could detect stimuli in the environment.
In your answer, use the words from the box below. (3)

receptor	**sensory neurone**	**brain**

....

....

....

....

....

1 Label the gland shown on the diagram and add the name of a hormone it produces. (2)

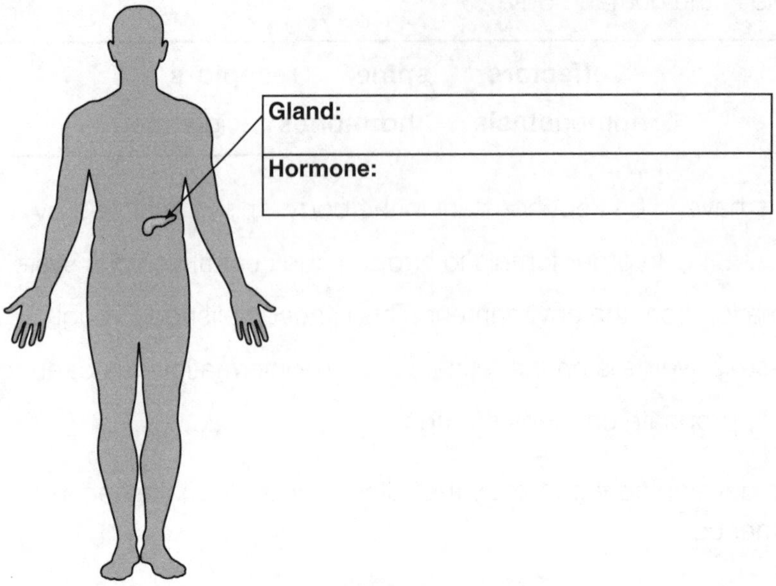

2 A new nanotechnology device has been developed for people with diabetes – it can detect levels of glucose in the blood and communicate this information to a hormone implant elsewhere in the body. The implant releases a precise quantity of hormone into the bloodstream when required.

(a) Explain how this device could help a person with type 1 diabetes who has just eaten a meal. (2)

....

....

(b) Explain why a person with type 2 diabetes might not have as much use for this technology. (2)

....

....

3 Complete the missing information in the table, which is about different endocrine glands in the body. (4)

Gland	Hormones produced
Pituitary gland	.... and ....
Pancreas	Insulin and glucagon
....	Thyroxine
....	Adrenaline
Ovary	.... and ....
Testes	Testosterone

1 The graph shows the thickness of the uterus during the menstrual cycle. Use the graph and your scientific knowledge to explain what happens in the woman's ovaries and uterus between days 5 and 28. (3)

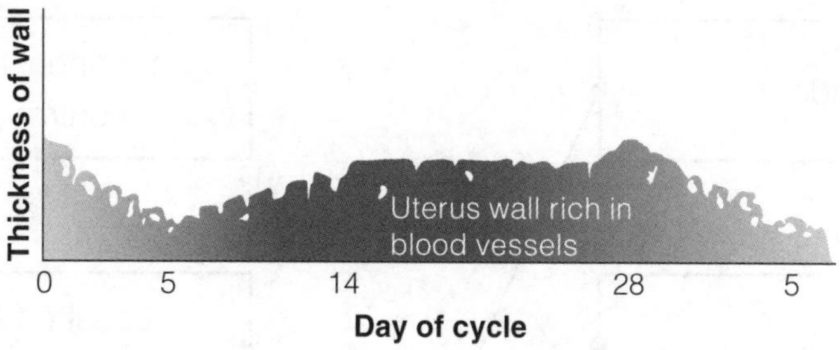

....

....

....

2 Match each hormone with the correct description. The first one has been done for you. (3)

FSH	Oestrogen	Progesterone	LH
promotes repair of the uterus wall **and** stimulates egg release.	maintains the lining of the uterus.	stimulates release of an egg **only**.	causes the egg to mature.

(Progesterone is joined to "maintains the lining of the uterus.")

3 During puberty, hormones cause changes in the bodies of both girls and boys. For example, girls begin producing eggs so that fertilisation can take place in order to produce a baby.

Describe **one** other change for girls and **one** change for boys, stating why the change occurs. (4)

Girls: ....

....

....

Boys: ....

....

....

1 **(a)** Draw a line to match each following method of contraception with the description that is most accurate.

One has been done for you: (3)

Condom	Permanent method of contraception
Intrauterine device	Least effective in preventing pregnancy
Sterilisation	Prevents implantation of embryo
Abstinence while egg is in oviduct	Most effective in preventing STIs

(b) A couple are deciding which method of contraception to use. They may want children in the future, but don't want the woman to suffer side effects from oral contraceptives. Which method is most suitable for giving maximum effectiveness? Give reasons for your answer. (3)

....

....

....

....

2 Explain how the contraceptive pill works.

In your answer, name any hormones involved. (2)

....

....

....

1 From the box below, choose **three** words to complete these sentences. (3)

zygotes	**gametes**	**diploid**	**haploid**	**mitosis**	**meiosis**

Eggs and sperm are .... They are .... because they contain one set of chromosomes. Eggs and sperm are produced in the ovaries and testes by ....

2 Tick (✓) the **two** statements about causes of variation that are true. (2)

Meiosis shuffles genes, which makes each gamete unique. ☐

Gametes fuse randomly. ☐

Zygotes fuse randomly. ☐

Mitosis shuffles genes, which makes each gamete the same. ☐

3

Sexual reproduction is the best strategy for organisms because it allows variation and therefore greater adaptation.

Asexual reproduction is better because when an organism is well adapted, it can produce exact copies of itself.

(a) John and Ayesha disagree about which type of reproduction is most beneficial to organisms. State which explanation, if any, is correct. Give the reasons for your choice. (3)

....

....

....

....

(b) Apart from variation, write down **one** other difference between sexual and asexual reproduction. (1)

....

....

(c) Describe how yeast carries out asexual reproduction. (2)

....

....

1 Tick (✓) the statements about the Human Genome Project (HGP) that are true. (3)

The genome of an organism is the entire genetic material present in its adult body cells. ☐

The data produced from the HGP produced a listing of amino acid sequences. ☐

The HGP involved collaboration between US and UK geneticists. ☐

The project allowed genetic abnormalities to be tracked between generations. ☐

The project was controversial as it relied on embryonic stem cells. ☐

2 Studies of genomes can help scientists work out the evolutionary history of organisms by comparing the similarity of particular DNA sequences that code for a specific protein.

The table shows the percentage DNA coding similarity for protein A in different organisms.

Species	% DNA coding similarity between species and humans for protein A
Human	100
Chimpanzee	100
Horse	88.5
Fish	78.6
Yeast	67.3
Protist	56.6

(a) What evidence is there in the table that closely related organisms developed from a recent common ancestor? (1)

....

(b) Using only the information from the table, which invertebrate is the most closely related to humans? .... (1)

3 The Human Genome Project has enabled specific genes to be identified that increase the risk of developing cancer in later life. Two of these genes are the *BRCA1* and *BRCA2* mutations that increase the risk of developing breast cancer.

(a) If women are prepared to take a genetic test, how could this information help doctors advise women about breast cancer? (2)

....

....

(b) If a woman possesses these mutations, it does not mean that she will definitely develop breast cancer. Why is this? (2)

....

....

1 The molecule DNA is a double helix made of two complementary strands.

(a) Write down the bases that pair with **T** and **C**. (1)

T pairs with ....

C pairs with ....

(b) How many bases code for **one** amino acid when a protein molecule is made? (1)

....

2 Raj is the owner of two dogs, both of which are about two years old. Both dogs are black in colour and came from the same litter of puppies.

(a) A dog's adult body cell contains 78 chromosomes.
How many chromosomes would be in a male dog's sperm cells? (1)

....

(b) The dogs' mother had white fur and the father had black fur.

Using what you know about dominant genes, suggest why there were no white puppies in the litter. (2)

....

....

3 Complete these two different crosses between a brown-eyed parent and a blue-eyed parent. (4)

(a)

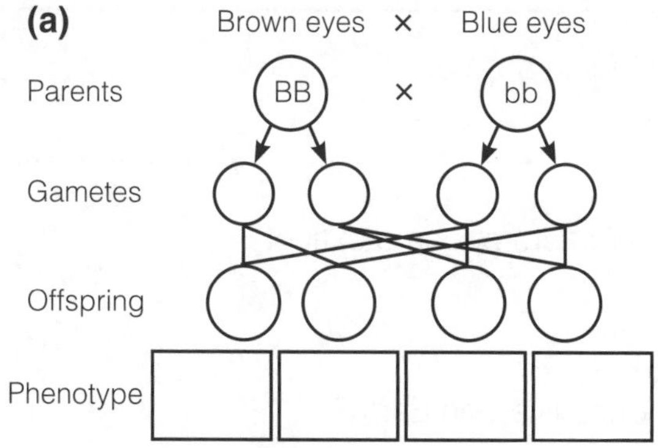

(b)

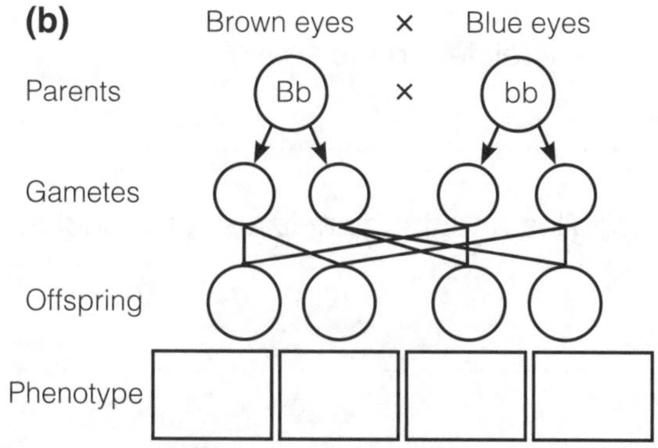

1 This is an evolutionary tree for some of our present-day vertebrates. Where possible, use the diagram to answer these questions.

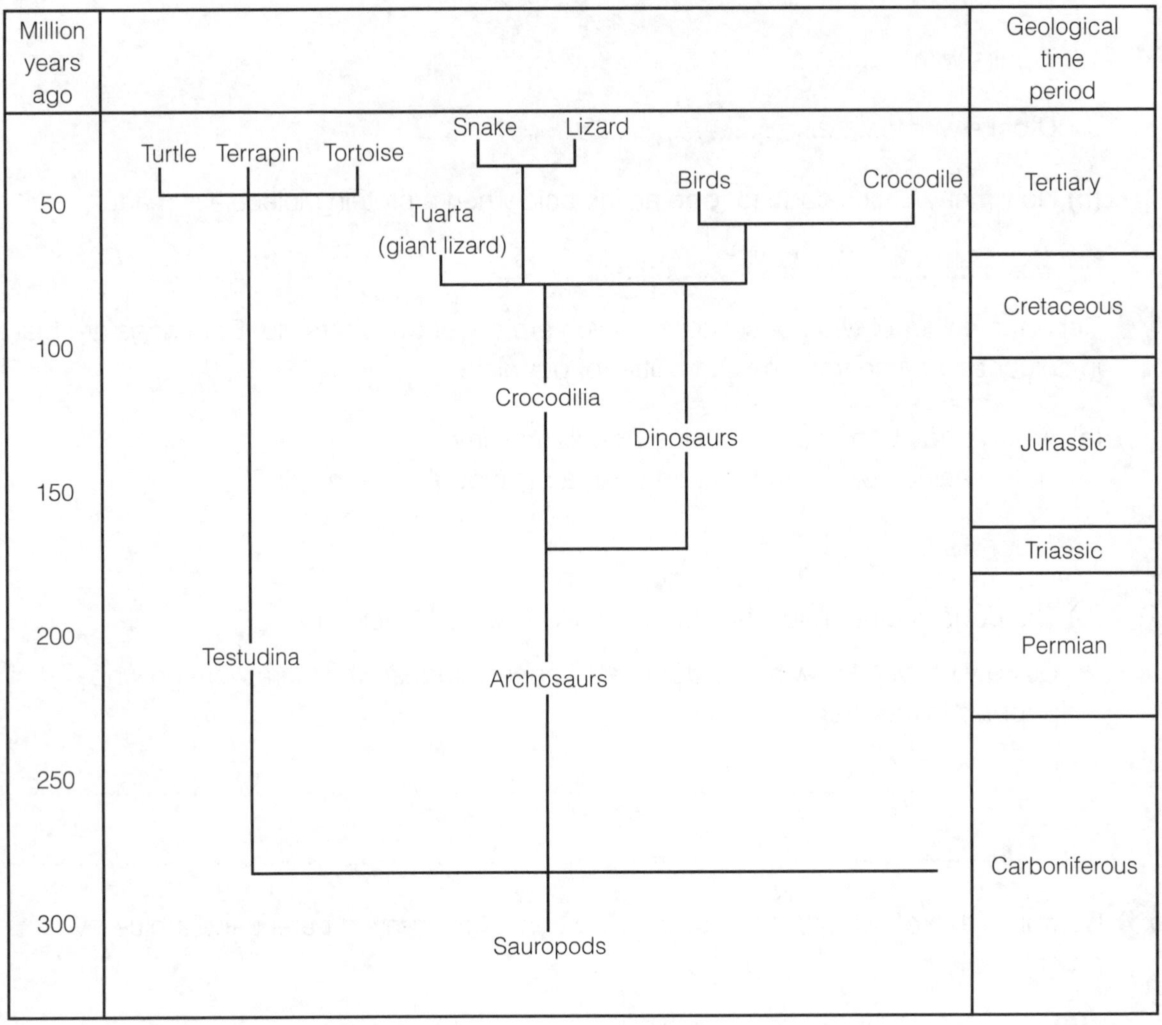

(a) How many millions of years ago did the testudina appear? (1)

....

(b) (i) In what geological time period did the dinosaurs become extinct? (1)

....

(ii) How do scientists know that dinosaurs once lived on Earth? (1)

....

(c) What group of animals alive today is most closely related to the snake? (1)

....

(d) Which ancestor is shared by dinosaurs, crocodiles and the giant lizard, but is not an ancestor of tortoises? (1)

....

1 Peppered moths are usually pale and speckled. They are often found amongst the lichens on silver birch tree bark.

The data below estimates the average number of peppered moths spotted in a city centre before and after the Industrial Revolution.

	Before Industrial Revolution		After Industrial Revolution	
Month	**Pale**	**Dark**	**Pale**	**Dark**
June	1261	102	87	1035
July	1247	126	108	1336
August	1272	93	72	1019

(a) Complete the table by calculating the mean number of each colour of moth during the summer months. (2)

Before Industrial Revolution		After Industrial Revolution	
Pale	**Dark**	**Pale**	**Dark**
....	....	....	....

(b) Draw a bar graph to represent your results. (2)

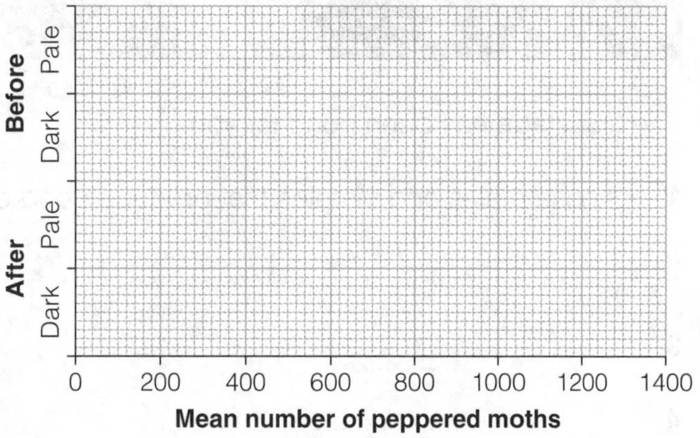

(c) Why do you think there were more pale-coloured moths than dark-coloured moths before the Industrial Revolution? (1)

....

(d) Explain why the number of dark-coloured peppered moths increased significantly during the Industrial Revolution. (2)

....

....

....

1 **(a)** A sheep farmer wants to breed sheep that grow high quality wool. What four stages of selective breeding can he use to produce his desired variety? (3)

The first stage has been done for you.

1. Choose males and females that produce good quality wool.

2. ....

3. ....

4. ....

(b) Apart from high quality wool, name another characteristic that a farmer might want to selectively breed into his flock. (1)

....

Selective breeding

Module 30

1 Describe how genetic engineering is different from selective breeding. (2)

....

....

....

2 Explain the benefit of each of these examples of genetic engineering.

(a) Resistance to herbicide in soya plants (1)

....

....

(b) Inserting beta-carotene genes into rice plants (1)

....

....

3 Some people think that genetically engineering resistance to herbicides in plants could have unforeseen consequences.

Give **one** example of a harmful effect. (1)

....

....

....

1 Lions, tigers and leopards are all carnivorous big cats. They have five toes on their front paws and four toes on their back paws. Their claws can be drawn back to avoid damage. They all roar. Tigers and leopards tend to be solitary animals but lions live in prides of females with one dominant male.

(a) Underline **one** piece of evidence from the information above that suggests that lions, tigers and leopards are all descended from a common ancestor. (1)

(b) This table shows how some scientists have named four species of large cat.

	Genus	Species
Lion	*Panthera*	*leo*
Tiger	*Panthera*	*tigris*
Leopard	*Panthera*	*pardus*
Snow leopard	*Uncia*	*uncia*

Are leopards more closely related to tigers or snow leopards? Explain your answer. (2)

....

....

....

2 Archaeopteryx is an ancient fossilised species of bird. When first discovered, scientists found it hard to classify.

Using features shown in the picture, explain why Archaeopteryx is difficult to classify. (2)

....

....

....

Classification

Module 32

1 Complete the following passage about adaptations using words from the box below. (3)

environment	**population**	**features**	**community**	**characteristics**
survival	**evolutionary**	**predatory**	**suited**	

Adaptations are special .... or .... that make a living organism particularly well .... to its .... Adaptations are part of an .... process that increases a living organism's chance of

....

2 A new species of insectivorous mammal has been discovered in Borneo. It has been observed in rainforest undergrowth and more open savannah-like areas. Scientists have called the creature a *long-nosed batink*. They have studied its diet and obtained this data.

Food	Ants	Termites	Aphids	Beetles	Maggots	Bugs	Grubs
Mass eaten per day / g	275	380	320	75	150	20	110

(a) Plot the data for termites, beetles, bugs and grubs as a bar chart. (3)

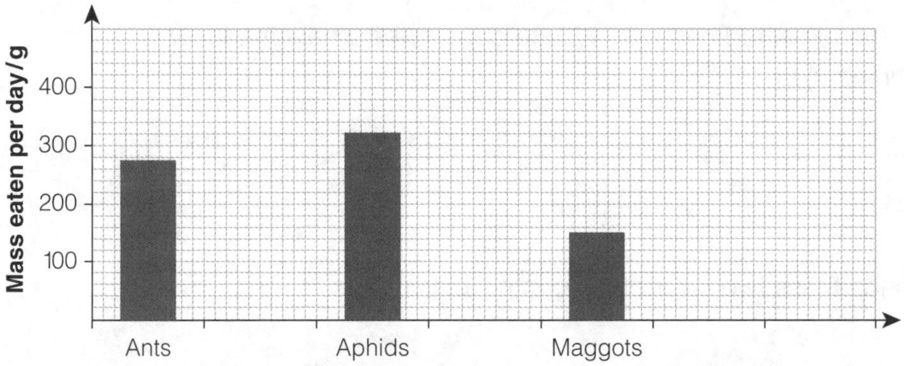

(b) Calculate the percentage of the batink's diet that is made up from termites. Show your working. (2)

.... %

(c) From what you know about the batink, suggest **two** behavioural adaptations it might have that makes it successful. (2)

....

....

Organisms and ecosystems

Module 33

1 A meadow supports a wide variety of animals and plants. George is carrying out a survey of the meadow to assess the populations of organisms found there.

(a) State the term that describes the meadow as a place for organisms to live. (1)

....

(b) Which word describes the different populations in the meadow and their interaction with the physical factors found there? (1)

....

(c) George has laid pitfall traps in the meadow to capture and count soil invertebrates. He notices that there are many flying insects that are too difficult to count and identify.

Suggest an item of apparatus he could use to survey the flying insects. (1)

....

(d) George uses a 0.25 m^2 quadrat to survey the plant populations. He lays ten quadrats in one corner of the field and finds a mean count of 16 meadow buttercups per quadrat. He estimates the area of the meadow to be 5000 m^2.

Calculate the expected number of buttercups in the whole meadow. Show your working. (2)

....

....

(e) George finds these two invertebrates in his pitfall traps.

Beetle

Snail

(i) The beetle feeds off other insects. Explain how a decrease in the number of beetles will eventually result in their numbers rising. (2)

....

....

(ii) Thrushes eat snails and worms. Describe what would happen to the number of snails if large numbers of thrushes arrived in their habitat. (1)

....

Module 34 Studying ecosystems

1 Apple trees are grown in orchards in temperate climates. They are part of a wider food web.

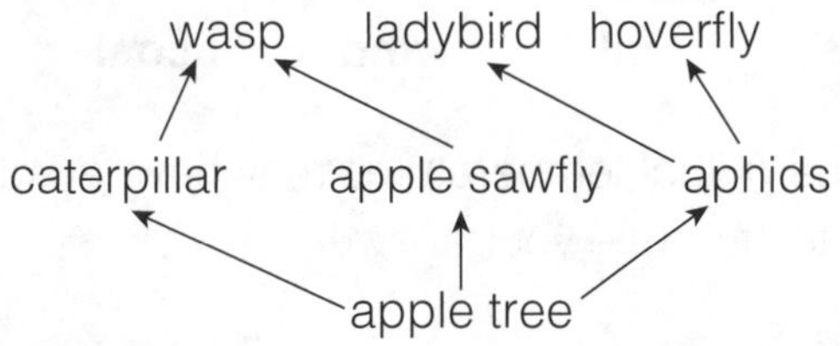

(a) The apple tree is a **producer**. What is meant by this term? (1)

....

(b) What is the source of energy for this food web? .... (1)

(c) Name a secondary consumer in the food web. .... (1)

2 Bird populations are a good indicator of environmental sustainability and allow scientists to track environmental changes in particular habitats.

Scientists measured the numbers of farmland birds and woodland birds in the UK between 1972 and 2002. The results are show below.

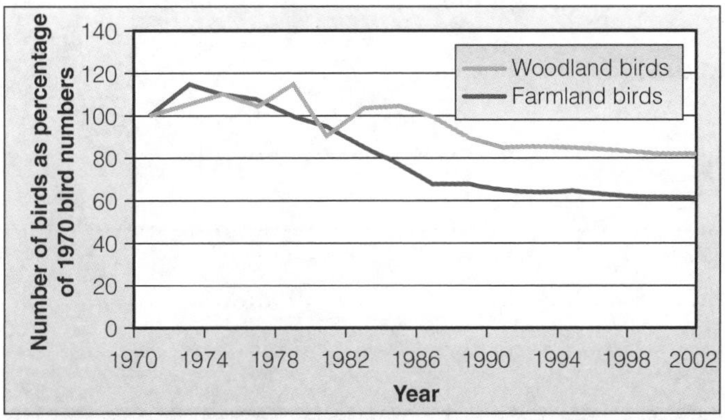

(a) Explain clearly how the numbers of farmland birds have changed between 1972 and 2002. (4)

....

....

....

....

(b) Suggest a reason for the overall change in numbers of farmland birds. (1)

....

(c) The government wants to reverse these changes by 2020. Suggest **one** thing it could do that would help to achieve this. (1)

....

Environmental change

Module 36

1 Circle the renewable resources. (1)

water **minerals** **oil** **wind** **coal** **wood**

2 Explain how rising average global temperatures may have an effect on the Earth. Use the headings below to structure your answer. (3)

Climate zones around the world:

....

....

....

Sea levels:

....

....

....

Ice caps and glaciers:

....

....

....

1 In Ireland, four species of bumble bee are now endangered. Scientists are worried that numbers may become so low that they are inadequate to provide pollination to certain plants.

State **two** reasons why some organisms become endangered. (2)

....

....

2 **(a)** What is deforestation? Tick (✓) the correct definition. (1)

Planting new trees ☐

Forest fires caused by hot weather ☐

Cutting down large areas of forest ☐

Polluting national parks with litter ☐

(b) Which of the following is a consequence of deforestation? Tick (✓) the correct answer. (1)

Decrease in soil erosion in tropical regions ☐

Increase in atmospheric carbon dioxide ☐

Increase in average rainfall ☐

Increase in habitat area ☐

3 Other than using wood for timber, give **two** other reasons for large-scale deforestation. (2)

....

....

4 Circle the correct options in the sentences below. (6)

When deforestation occurs in **tropical / arctic / desert** regions, it has a devastating impact on the environment.

The loss of **trees / animals / insects** means less photosynthesis takes place, so less **oxygen / nitrogen / carbon dioxide** is removed from the atmosphere.

It also leads to a reduction in **variation / biodiversity / mutation**, because some species may become **protected / damaged / extinct** and **habitats / land / farms** are destroyed.

5 Sometimes when land has been cleared of forests to grow crops, farmers stop producing good yields after a few years. Explain why. (1)

....

....

1 Choose the correct words from the list to complete this paragraph on the water cycle: (3)

boiled	**precipitation**	**rivers**	**organisms**	**evaporated**	**condensation**

The water cycle provides fresh water for .... on land before draining into the seas. Water is .... from seawater to form vapour in the atmosphere. This vapour then forms clouds and falls as ....

2 A group of students wanted to investigate factors affecting decay. They mixed soil with small discs cut from leaves. They divided the leaf disc / soil mixture equally into four test tubes, as shown below.

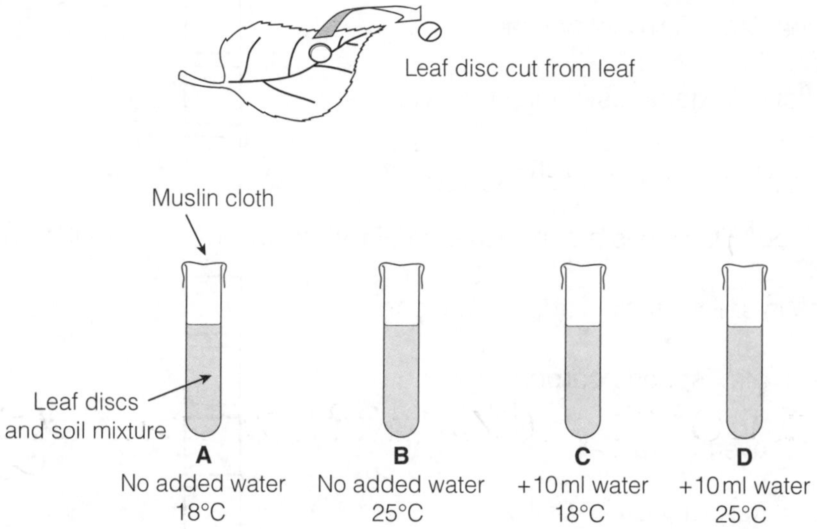

(a) In which tube would you expect the leaf discs to decay fastest? Give a reason for your answer. .... (2)

....

(b) The students did not add any microorganisms to the test tubes. Where will the microorganisms that cause decay come from? (1)

....

(c) Why did the students seal the tubes with muslin cloth instead of a rubber bung? (1)

....

(d) Suggest **one** way in which the students could use the leaf discs to measure the rate of decay. (1)

....

1 The chemical sodium chloride is more commonly known as 'salt' (i.e. the food flavouring).

Sodium chloride can be made in the laboratory by reacting sodium with chlorine gas. Salt is very soluble in water.

(a) Give the chemical symbols for the two elements present in sodium chloride. Use the periodic table on page 192 to help you. (2)

NaCl

(b) Write a word equation to show the reaction between sodium and chlorine to produce sodium chloride. (2)

Sodium + chloride → Sodium chloride

(c) Is sodium chloride a mixture or a compound? Explain your answer. (2)

Compound, there chemically combined in fixed position

(d) When salt dissolves in water, does it form a mixture or a compound? Explain your answer. (2)

mixture, you can seperate without chemical mixture.

(e) A student wants to separate salt and water from salty water. Which two methods of separation listed below would be appropriate for the student to use? Tick the relevant box or boxes. (2)

Filtration	☐	Simple distillation	☑
Crystallisation	☑	Chromatography	☐

Atoms and the periodic table

Module 39

1 One of the early representations of the atom, the 'plum pudding' model, was further developed in light of Rutherford, Geiger and Marsden's scattering experiment. This led to the conclusion that the positive charge of an atom is contained within a small volume known as the nucleus. Niels Bohr improved this model and it is this model that forms the basis of the way in which we represent the structure of atoms today.

The plum pudding model

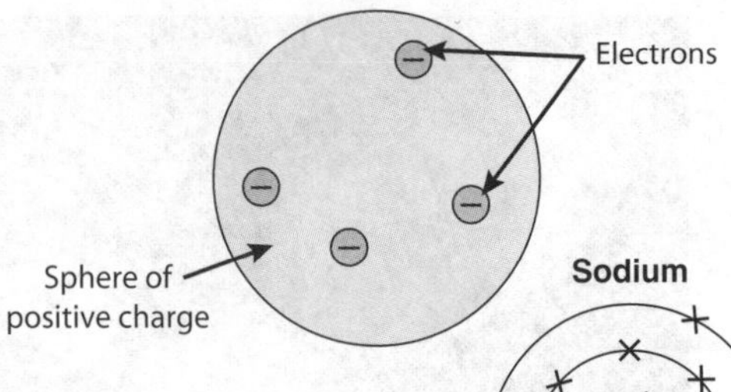

Sodium

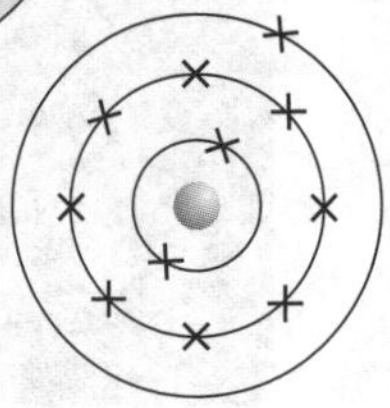

The plum pudding version of an atom is shown above.

Today, an atom such as sodium is represented by a diagram like the one above.

(a) Give **two** differences between the 'plum pudding' model of an atom and today's model. (2)

Plum pudding dosen't show Nucleus or electron orbits.

(b) What observation in Rutherford, Geiger and Marsden's scattering experiment led them to conclude that the positive charge of an atom was contained in a small volume? (1)

most went stright through the thin piece of gold.

(c) What improvements did Niels Bohr make to the nuclear model and what evidence did he have to support these changes? (2)

electrons orbit the Nucleus at specific distance. experimental evidence.

(d) James Chadwick developed the idea that the nucleus of an atom contains protons and neutrons.

Complete the table below showing the properties of the sub-atomic particles. (4)

Particle	Relative charge	Relative mass
Proton	+ 1	1
Neutron	0	1
Electron	- 1	very small

(e) An atom of sodium contains 11 protons, 12 neutrons and 11 electrons.

(i) What is the atomic number of sodium? 11 (1)

(ii) What is the mass number of sodium? 23 (1)

Atomic structure

Module 40

1 The diagrams below represent an atom of magnesium and an atom of fluorine:

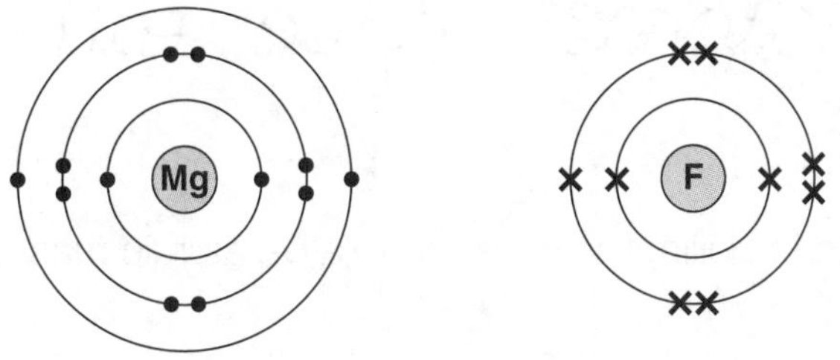

The electronic structure of magnesium can also be written as 2,8,2

(a) How many shells of electrons does a magnesium atom have? (1)

3

(b) What is the electronic structure of fluorine? (1)

2,7

(c) In which group of the periodic table would you expect to find fluorine? Explain your answer. (2)

Group 7 because it has 7 electrons on the outer shell.

2 Dmitri Mendeleev is often referred to as the father of the periodic table, as he was instrumental in its construction.

Mendeleev placed the metals lithium and sodium in the same group of the periodic table.

(a) How are the elements arranged in the periodic table? (1)

Order of increasing atomic (proton) Number.

(b) Explain why Mendeleev placed sodium and lithium in the same group of the periodic table. (1)

Same amount of electron on Outer shell

(c) Give **two** characteristic properties of metals. (2)

1 **(a)** Explain why the noble gases are chemically inert. (2)

Their atoms have full outer Shells

(b) What is the trend in boiling point as the relative atomic mass of the noble gases increases? .... (1)

2 The element sodium reacts vigorously with water. When universal indicator solution is added to the resulting solution a colour change is observed.

(a) Write a balanced symbol equation for the reaction between sodium and water. (2)

....

(b) What colour would universal indicator solution turn when it is added to the resulting solution? Explain your answer. (2)

....

....

(c) The element potassium reacts more vigorously with water than sodium. Explain why. (2)

The outer shell gets futher away from the positive attraction of the nucleus.

3 Sodium reacts with bromine gas as shown by the equation below:

.........$Na_{(s)}$ + ...$Cl_{2(g)}$ $\longrightarrow$ ....$NaCl_{(s)}$

(a) Balance the above equation. (2)

(b) What type of bonding is present in sodium chloride (NaCl)? (1)

....

(c) When chlorine gas is bubbled through sodium bromide solution a chemical reaction occurs. Write a word equation for this reaction. (2)

....

(d) What name is given to the type of reaction that occurs when chlorine gas reacts with sodium bromide solution? Explain why the reaction occurs. (2)

....

....

1 Consider the structures of sodium (Na), chlorine (Cl_2) and sodium chloride (NaCl).

Draw arrows from each substance to its correct structure. One structure will not have an arrow drawn to it. (3)

Sodium	Ionic
Chlorine	Simple molecular
Sodium chloride	Giant molecular
	Metallic

2 Calcium reacts with oxygen to form calcium oxide. The bonding in calcium oxide is ionic.

(a) Complete the diagrams below to show the electronic configurations and charges of the calcium and oxygen ions. (2)

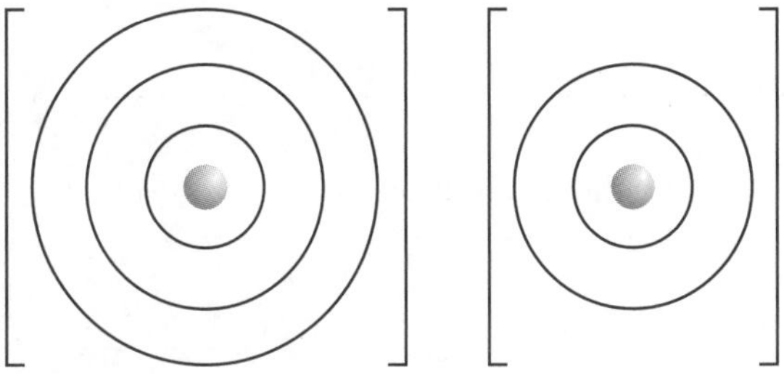

(b) State the charges on each ion. (2)

....

....

3 **(a)** Draw a dot-and-cross diagram to show the bonding in HCl. (1)

(b) The dot-and-cross diagram for a molecule of oxygen is shown below.

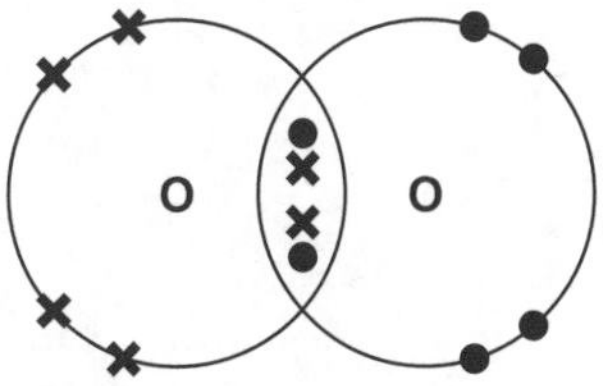

How many covalent bonds are there between the two oxygen atoms? (1)

....

1 The structure of calcium oxide is shown below.

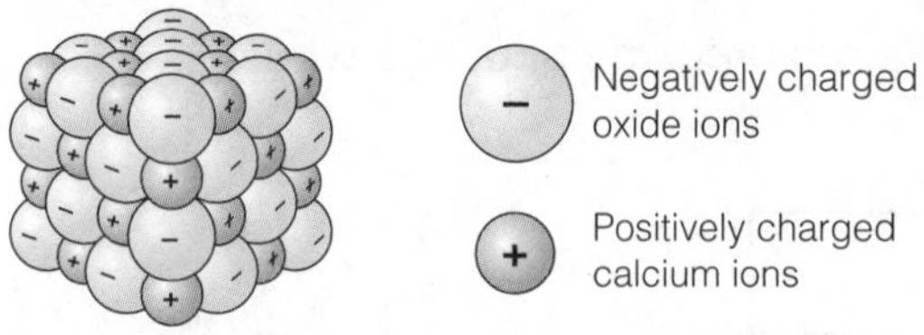

(a) What force holds the ions in place in calcium oxide? (1)

Electrostatic forces of attraction

(b) What is the empirical formula of calcium oxide? Explain your answer. (2)

CaO

2 The structure of a covalent compound is shown below.

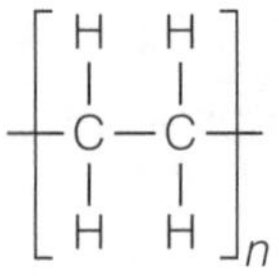

(a) Name this type of structure. .... (1)

(b) What is the empirical formula of this structure? Explain your answer. (2)

3 Part of the structure of boron nitride is shown below.

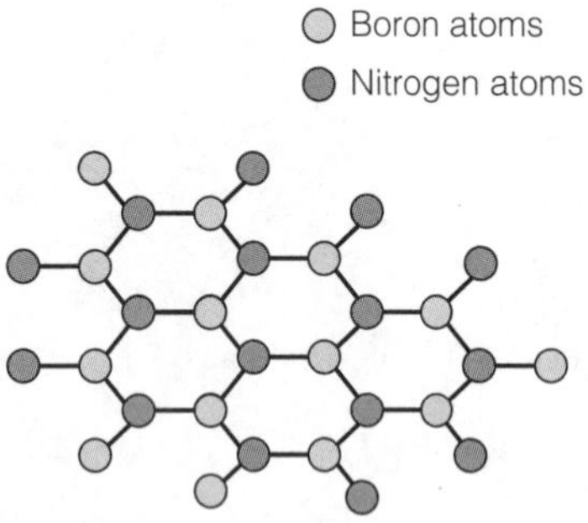

What type of structure does boron nitride have? Explain your answer. (2)

Ball and stick

1 Solids, liquids and gases are the three main states of matter. The three physical states of matter can be easily interconverted.

(a) Draw a diagram to show the arrangement of particles in a solid. (2)

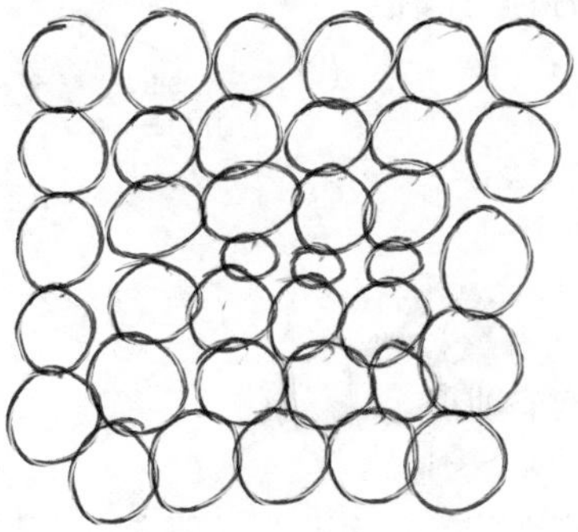

(b) What forces are broken when a solid turns into a liquid? (1)

....

2 Consider the table below, which provides information about the physical properties of two materials.

	Material A	Material B
Melting point/°C	801	3730
Electrical conductivity of solid	Poor	Poor
Electrical conductivity of liquid	Good	Poor

(a) Material A has a giant ionic structure. Explain how this can be deduced from the table. (1)

....

(b) Explain why material A is a poor conductor of electricity in the solid state. (2)

....

....

(c) Deduce the structure of material B. Explain your answer. (2)

....

....

(d) Explain why material B is a poor conductor of electricity in both the solid and liquid states. (2)

....

....

1 The diagram shows the structure of a metal such as magnesium.

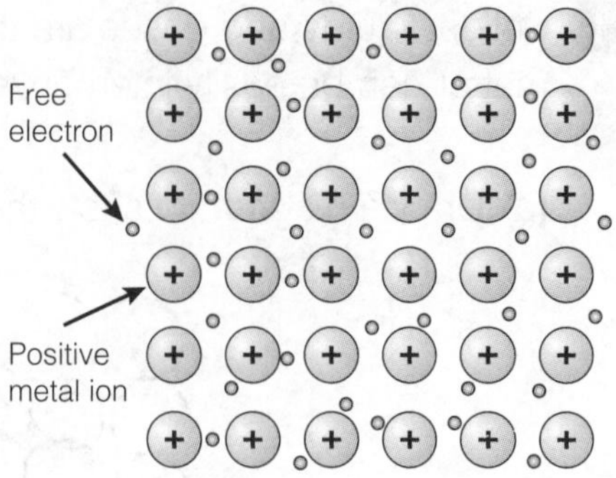

With reference to the diagram, explain the following:

(a) Why metals are malleable (i.e. able to be bent and shaped). (2)

....

....

(b) Why metals usually have high melting points. (2)

....

....

(c) Why metals are good conductors of electricity. (2)

....

....

2 Most metals in everyday use are alloys, such as steel.

(a) What is an alloy? (1)

....

(b) With reference to its structure, explain why most alloys are harder than pure metals. (2)

....

....

3 This question is about different structures of carbon.

(a) Give **two** uses of fullerenes. (2)

....

....

(b) State **two** properties of fullerenes. (2)

....

....

(c) What is the difference between a fullerene and a carbon nanotube? (1)

....

1 Consider the equation below.

$2Al_{(s)} + Fe_2O_{3(l)} \longrightarrow Al_2O_{3(s)} + 2Fe_{(l)}$

(a) With reference to the above equation, what do you understand by the term 'conservation of mass'? (1)

....

(b) Complete the table below by filling in the relative atomic (A_r) or formula (M_r) mass of each substance in the equation. (4)

Substance	A_r / M_r
Al	
Fe_2O_3	
Al_2O_3	
Fe	

2 Magnesium oxide can be made by heating magnesium in air or by the thermal decomposition of magnesium carbonate.

(a) Explain why the mass of magnesium increases when it is burnt in air. (2)

....

....

(b) Write a balanced symbol equation for the reaction that occurs when magnesium is heated in air. (2)

....

(c) Explain why the mass of magnesium carbonate decreases when it is heated in air. (2)

....

....

(d) Write a balanced symbol equation for the thermal decomposition of magnesium carbonate. (2)

....

Mass and equations

Module 47

1 A student weighed out a 3 cm piece magnesium on a balance that reads to 0.01g.

He then added the magnesium to 25 cm^3 of hydrochloric acid that was measured out using a measuring cylinder that has graduations at every 1 cm^3.

(a) What is the uncertainty of the mass reading? (1)

....

(b) What values does the true volume of hydrochloric acid used lie between?

Explain your answer. (2)

....

....

....

2 Solution A has a concentration of 45 g/dm^3. Solution B contains 12g of solute dissolved in 225 cm^3 of water.

(a) What is meant by the term 'solute'? (1)

....

(b) How many grams of solute are present in 600 cm^3 of solution A? (1)

....

(c) What is the concentration of solution B in g/dm^3? (1)

....

(d) Does 500 cm^3 of solution A or B contain the most particles?

Explain your answer. (2)

....

....

....

1 Calcium reacts with oxygen present in the air to form calcium oxide.

(a) Write a word equation for this reaction. (2)

....

(b) Explain why this is an oxidation reaction. (2)

....

....

(c) Name a metal that could be used to displace calcium from calcium oxide. Explain your choice of metal. (2)

....

....

(d) Write a word equation for this reaction. (2)

....

(e) In your equation from part **d**, give the name of the substance that has been reduced. (1)

....

2 Many metals are found in the Earth's crust as ores. For example, haematite is an ore containing iron(III) oxide (Fe_2O_3); bauxite is an ore containing aluminium oxide (Al_2O_3). Both metals can be extracted from their ores by reduction.

(a) What process is used to extract metals above carbon in the reactivity series from their ores? .... (1)

(b) When iron(III) oxide is reduced by carbon, iron and carbon dioxide are formed. Write a balanced symbol equation for this reaction. (2)

....

(c) Explain why aluminium cannot be extracted from its ore by reduction with carbon. (2)

....

....

(d) When aluminium is extracted from its ore during electrolysis the following reaction occurs:

aluminium oxide $\longrightarrow$ aluminium + oxygen

Which substance is reduced in this reaction? Explain your answer. (2)

....

....

1. Zinc, zinc oxide and zinc carbonate all react with acids.

(a) Name the salt formed when zinc, zinc oxide and zinc carbonate react with sulfuric acid. (1)

....

(b) Write a word equation for the reaction between zinc oxide and hydrochloric acid. (2)

....

(c) State **two** observations that would be seen when zinc carbonate reacts with nitric acid. (2)

....

....

(d) Name and give the formula of the gas formed when zinc carbonate reacts with nitric acid. (2)

....

(e) Explain why no fizzing or bubbling is observed when zinc oxide reacts with sulfuric acid. (1)

....

2. Copper(II) oxide (CuO) reacts with sulfuric acid to make the soluble salt copper(II) sulfate according to the equation below.

$$CuO_{(s)} + H_2SO_{4(aq)} \longrightarrow CuSO_{4(aq)} + H_2O_{(l)}$$

(a) Describe the steps you would take to prepare a sample of solid copper(II) sulfate, starting from copper(II) oxide and sulfuric acid solution. (3)

....

....

....

(b) The salt sodium nitrate can be formed by the reaction of sodium carbonate with an acid. Name this acid. (1)

....

Module 50 Reactions of acids

1 Hydrogen chloride (HCl) and ethanoic acid (CH_3COOH) both dissolve in water to form acidic solutions.

(a) What is the pH range of acids? (1)

....

(b) Give the name and formula for the ion present in solutions of hydrogen chloride and ethanoic acid. (2)

....

(c) What is the common name for hydrogen chloride solution? (1)

....

(d) Acids can be neutralised by reaction with an alkali such as sodium hydroxide.

Write an ionic equation for the reaction that occurs when an acid is neutralised by an alkali. Include state symbols in your equation. (2)

....

(e) What colour would methyl orange turn when added to a solution of ethanoic acid? (1)

....

2 Draw line to match each word with its meaning. (6)

Cation	The liquid or solution containing ions that is broken down during electrolysis
Anion	The positive electrode
Anode	The separating of chemicals using electricity
Cathode	A negative ion
Electrolysis	The negative electrode
Electrolyte	A positive ion

1 The diagram shows how a molten salt such as lead(II) bromide ($PbBr_2$) can be electrolysed. Lead(II) bromide consists of Pb^{2+} and Br^- ions.

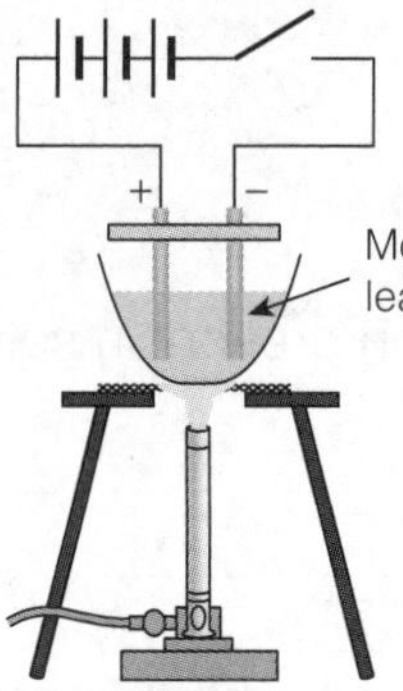

(a) What general name is given to positive ions? (1)

....

(b) What general name is given to negative ions?

.... (1)

(c) Explain why the lead(II) bromide needs to be molten. (2)

....

....

2 **(a)** The table below shows the products at each electrode when the following solutions are electrolysed.

Some answers have already been filled in.
Complete the table. (6)

Solution	Product at anode	Product at cathode
NaCl	H_2	
KNO_3		
$CuSO_4$		
Water diluted with sulfuric acid		O_2

(b) Explain why sodium is not formed at the cathode when aqueous sodium chloride is electrolysed. (2)

....

....

Module 52 Applications of electrolysis

1 In an experiment a pupil adds a sample of a salt to a beaker of water, stirs the mixture until all of the salt has dissolved and records the temperature change. Her results are shown below:

- Initial temperature of water: 21°C
- Final temperature of water: 18.5°C

(a) Calculate the temperature change. (1)

....

(b) Does this experiment show an exothermic or endothermic change? Explain your answer. (2)

....

....

(c) What happens to the temperature of the surroundings during this experiment? (1)

....

2 When methane burns in air an exothermic reaction takes place. The equation for the reaction is shown here:

$CH_{4(g)} + 2O_{2(g)} \longrightarrow CO_{2(g)} + 2H_2O_{(l)}$

(a) On the axes, draw and label a reaction profile for an exothermic reaction. Label the reactants, products, activation energy and the overall energy change. (5)

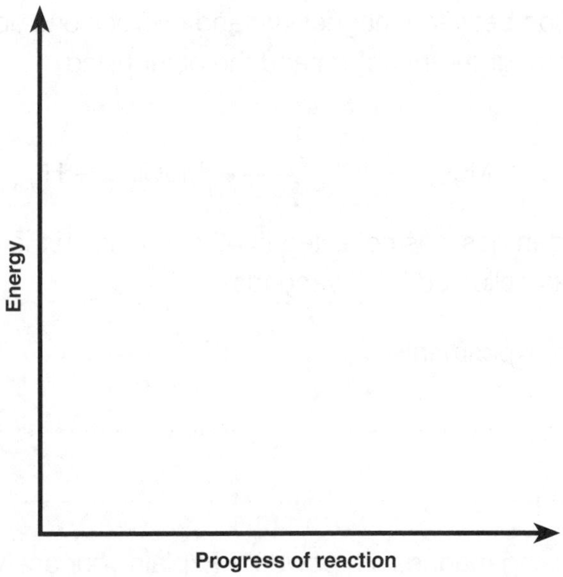

(b) Give an example of an endothermic chemical reaction. (1)

....

1 A pupil was investigating the effect of temperature on the rate of reaction between aqueous sodium thiosulfate with dilute hydrochloric acid. When the acid is added to the sodium thiosulfate solution, a precipitate of sulfur gradually forms. The pupil recorded the time taken for a cross written on a piece of paper to disappear from view.

The experiment was repeated at different temperatures. The results are shown in the table below.

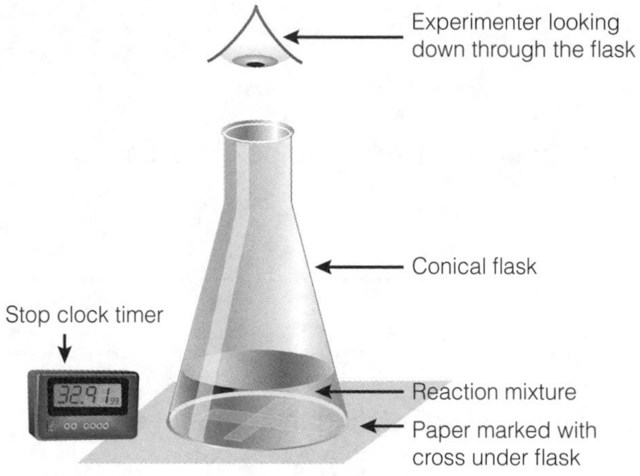

Temperature (°C)	Time taken for cross to disappear from view (s)
15	70
25	44
40	30
55	22
70	14

(a) At which temperature was the reaction the fastest? .... (1)

(b) Suggest how the rate of this reaction at 30°C will change when the concentration of hydrochloric acid is increased. Explain your answer. (2)

....

....

2 A student investigating the rate of reaction between magnesium and hydrochloric acid carried out two experiments: one using magnesium ribbon and the other using magnesium powder.

The equation for the reaction is shown here: $Mg_{(s)} + 2HCl_{(aq)} \longrightarrow MgCl_{2(aq)} + H_{2(g)}$

In the first experiment, 69 cm^3 of hydrogen gas was collected in 46 seconds. In the second experiment, 18 cm^3 of hydrogen gas was collected in 10 seconds.

(a) Calculate the rate of reaction in both experiments. (3)

....

....

(b) Which experiment was carried out using magnesium powder? Explain your answer. (2)

....

1 **(a)** Adding a catalyst to a reaction increases the rate of reaction. Draw, on the diagram below, the reaction profile for the reaction when a catalyst is added. (1)

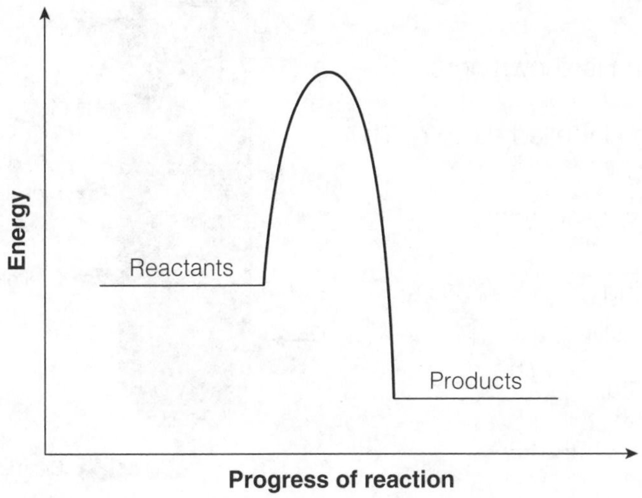

(b) Explain how a catalyst is able to increase the rate of a reaction. (2)

....

....

2 In an experiment, a student heated some blue crystals of hydrated copper(II) sulfate in an evaporating dish.

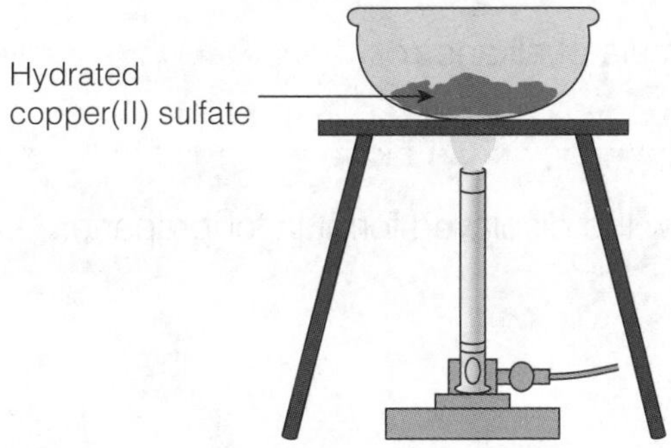

(a) State what colour change will be observed during the reaction. (1)

....

(b) Write a word equation for the change that occurs to the hydrated copper(II) sulfate during this experiment. (2)

....

(c) Describe what will be observed when water is added to the solid remaining at the end of the experiment. (1)

....

(d) Is the addition of water an exothermic or endothermic reaction? (1)

....

1 Crude oil is separated into its constituent components by fractional distillation. A fractionating column is used to carry out fractional distillation.

A diagram of a fractionating column is shown here.

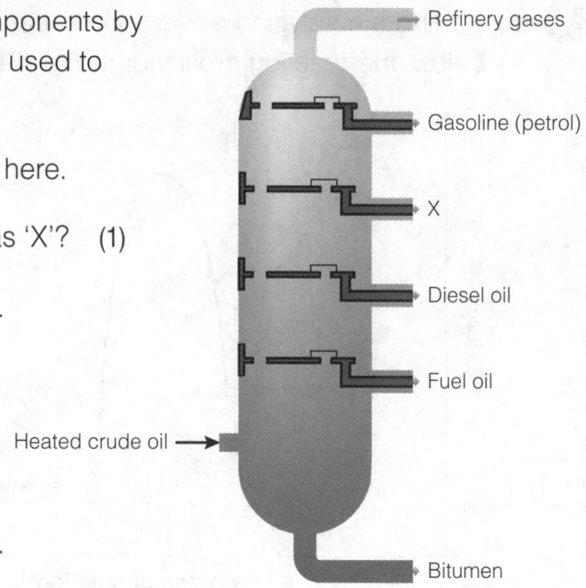

(a) What is the name of the fraction labelled as 'X'? (1)

....

(b) As you go down the fractionating column, what happens to the boiling point of the fractions? (1)

....

(c) Explain how crude oil is separated in a fractionating column. (3)

....

....

....

2 Most of the hydrocarbons found in crude oil are members of the homologous series of hydrocarbons called the alkanes.

(a) What is the general formula of alkanes? (1)

....

(b) In the space below, draw the displayed formula for propane. (1)

(c) What is the molecular formula of the member of the homologous series after propane? (1)

....

(d) Other than the same general formula, give one other feature of a homologous series. (1)

....

Crude oil, hydrocarbons and alkanes

Module 56

1 Propane (C_3H_8) is an alkane frequently bottled and used as a fuel.

(a) Name the products produced when propane undergoes complete combustion. (2)

....

....

(b) Write a balanced symbol equation for the complete combustion of propane. (2)

....

....

(c) In the complete combustion of propane which substance has been oxidised? (1)

....

2 Cracking is a method of converting long-chain hydrocarbons into shorter, more useful hydrocarbons.

(a) Name a catalyst used to crack hydrocarbons. (1)

....

(b) Other than use of a catalyst, state an alternative method for cracking hydrocarbons. (2)

....

....

(c) The equation for a reaction that occurs during this process is:

$$C_{12}H_{26} \longrightarrow C_2H_4 + C_6H_{12} + X$$

In the balanced equation, what is the molecular formula of X? (1)

....

(d) Describe how the gas collected during cracking can be shown to contain a double bond. (2)

....

....

1 Paint and household cleaning chemicals are typical examples of everyday chemical formulations.

(a) What is a formulation? (1)

....

(b) Are formulations chemically pure? Explain your answer. (2)

....

....

(c) Give **one** other example of a type of formulation. (1)

....

2 Pen ink is typically a mixture of dyes. The individual dyes in pen ink can be separated by paper chromatography. The chromatogram below is for an unknown ink 'X' and the standard colours blue, red and green.

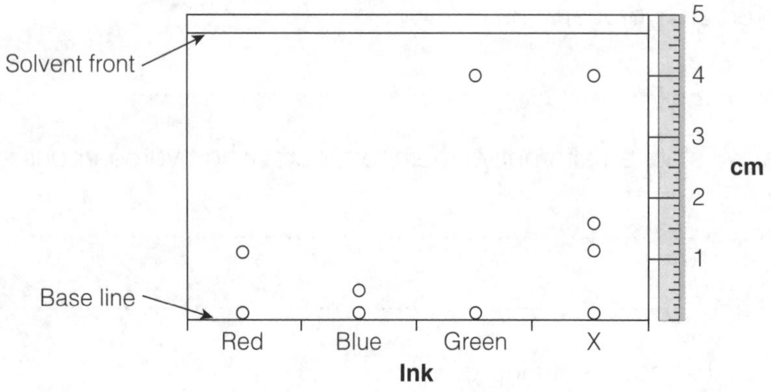

(a) What is the mobile phase in paper chromatography? (1)

....

(b) Which colours are present in ink X?

Explain your answer. (2)

....

....

(c) Calculate the R_f for the blue ink. (2)

....

....

1 When carbon dioxide gas is bubbled through limewater the following reaction occurs:

$$Ca(OH)_{2(aq)} + CO_{2(g)} \longrightarrow CaCO_{3(s)} + H_2O_{(l)}$$

(a) What is the chemical name for limewater? (1)

....

(b) With reference to the above equation, explain why limewater turns cloudy when carbon dioxide is bubbled through it. (2)

....

....

2 **(a)** Describe what would be observed when moist blue litmus paper is added to a gas jar containing chlorine gas. (2)

....

....

(b) Is chlorine an acidic or alkaline gas?

What evidence is there to support your answer? (2)

....

....

3 Hydrogen and oxygen gases are both colourless, odourless gases.

(a) What is the chemical test and observation for hydrogen gas? (2)

....

....

(b) What is the chemical test and observation for oxygen gas? (2)

....

....

(c) When hydrogen gas burns in air it reacts with oxygen to form water. Write a balanced symbol equation for the reaction taking place. (2)

....

....

1 Many scientists think that the Earth's early atmosphere may have been similar in composition to the gases typically released by volcanoes today.

The pie charts below show the composition of the atmosphere today and the composition of gases released by a volcano.

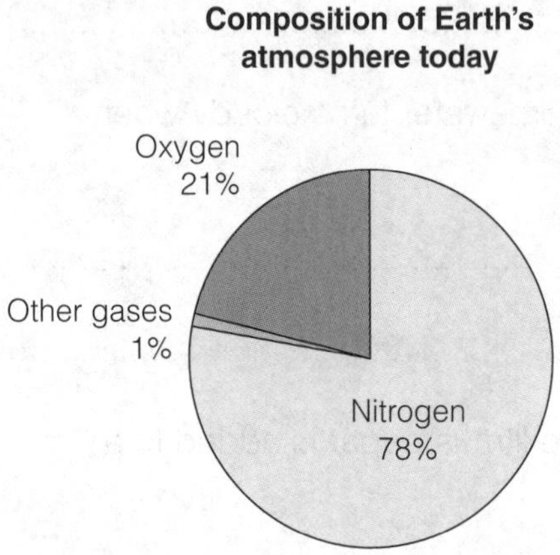

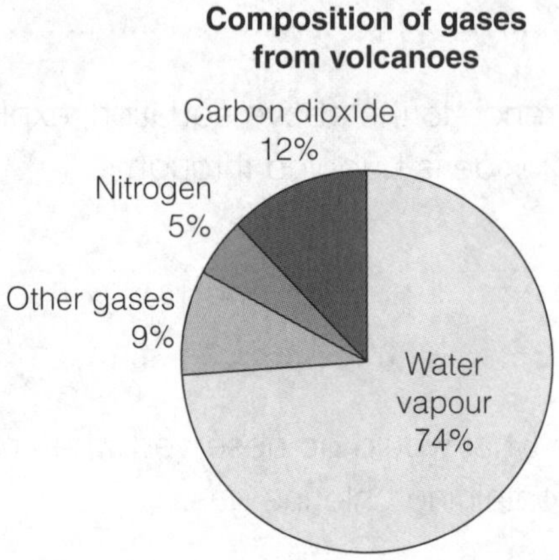

(a) Name a gas that is more abundant in the Earth's atmosphere today than in the early atmosphere. (1)

....

(b) Why is the amount of water vapour in the atmosphere significantly less now than in the early atmosphere? (2)

....

....

(c) Describe the process that caused the percentage of oxygen in the atmosphere to increase. (2)

....

....

(d) Outline **two** ways in which the amount of carbon dioxide in the early atmosphere decreased. (2)

....

....

1 When fossil fuels are burnt, carbon dioxide gas is produced and released into the atmosphere. Some people believe carbon dioxide to be a greenhouse gas.

(a) Explain how greenhouse gases maintain the temperature on Earth. (2)

(b) Name **one** other greenhouse gas. (1)

(c) Outline **two** ways in which human activity increases the amounts of greenhouse gases in the atmosphere. (2)

(d) Why is it not easy to predict the impact of changes on global climate change? (2)

(e) Describe **two** potential effects of increasing average global temperature. (2)

(f) Describe **two** forms of global action that can be taken to reduce the carbon footprint. (2)

(g) Outline **two** potential problems that governments might face when trying to reduce the carbon footprint. (2)

1 The combustion of fossil fuels, e.g. from cars, is a major source of atmospheric pollution.

(a) What is meant by a fossil fuel? (1)

....

(b) How are carbon and carbon monoxide formed from the combustion of fossil fuels? (1)

....

(c) State **one** harmful effect caused by the release of oxides of nitrogen into the atmosphere. (1)

....

(d) Give two detrimental consequences of releasing particulates into the air. (2)

....

....

(e) Explain why carbon monoxide is a toxic gas. (2)

....

....

(f) Fuels can contain sulfur as an impurity. Explain how burning this impurity can cause problems in the environment. (3)

....

....

....

1 We use the Earth's resources to provide us with warmth, shelter, food and transport. As the Earth is a finite source of resources, we need to ensure that we use them sustainably.

(a) What is sustainable development? (1)

....

(b) What is meant by the term 'potable water'? (1)

....

(c) After identification of an appropriate source of fresh water, what two stages then need to occur to turn this into potable water? (2)

....

....

(d) Outline the processes that are used to treat sewage. (3)

....

....

....

2 Salty water, e.g. seawater, can be desalinated (i.e. treated to reduce its salt content). One such method is distillation.

(a) In the space below, draw a labelled diagram to show how seawater can be distilled. Describe how distillation produces desalinated water. (5)

....

....

(b) What method of desalination involves the use of membranes? (1)

....

Life-cycle assessment and recycling

Module 64

1 Life-cycle assessments (LCAs) are carried out to evaluate the environmental impact of products at different stages of the life of a product.

(a) Other than transport and distribution, state **two** other stages of a product life cycle that will be considered when carrying out an LCA. (2)

....

....

(b) State **two** quantities that are considered when conducting an LCA. (2)

....

....

(c) Explain why the pollution value in a life-cycle value may result in the LCA not being totally objective. (2)

....

....

(d) Why might selective or abbreviated LCAs be misused? (1)

....

2 The table below shows an example of an LCA for the use of plastic (polythene) and paper shopping bags.

	Amounts per 1000 bags over the whole LCA	
	Paper	**Plastic (polythene)**
Energy use (mJ)	2590	713
Fossil fuel use (kg)	28	12.8
Solid waste (kg)	34	6
Greenhouse gas emissions (kg CO_2)	72	36
Fresh water use (litres)	3387	198

Based on the above figures, why might some people think that plastic (polythene) bags should be used instead of paper bags? Use information from the table in your answer. (3)

....

....

....

1 Neil, an astronaut, has a mass of 78 kg.

(a) Calculate Neil's weight.

(gravitational field strength = 10 N/kg) (1)

~~78×10~~ 78kg × 10N/Kg = 780N

(b) The Moon has a gravitational field strength of 1.6 N/kg.

What would Neil's mass and weight be on the Moon? (2)

....

....

(c) Neil also has a gravitational field that causes attraction.

Explain why this has no measurable effect on either the Moon or the Earth. (2)

....

....

2 The diagram shows Louise, a runner.

(a) Calculate the resultant force acting on Louise. (2)

120 + 30 = 150N

....

(b) The forces on Louise changed as shown by the diagram below.

(i) What is the resultant force on Louise now? (1)

90+90=180N

(ii) What statement can be made about her speed now? Explain your answer. (2)

....

....

(c) Louise uses 90 N of force and the work done is 25 kJ. What distance does she cover? (2)

90N × 25KN = 2,250J

....

Forces | Module 65

1 The graph below shows the results of an extension of a spring in response to different forces.

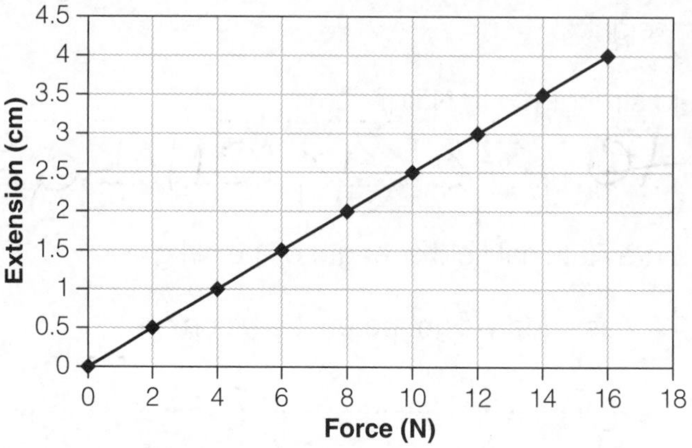

(a) What term is given to the relationship shown in this graph? (1)

linear.

(b) Calculate the spring constant for this spring. (3)

$\frac{2}{0.5} = 4$ N/cm

(c) The results were repeated, but with a larger range of masses providing the force. The results are shown in the graph below.

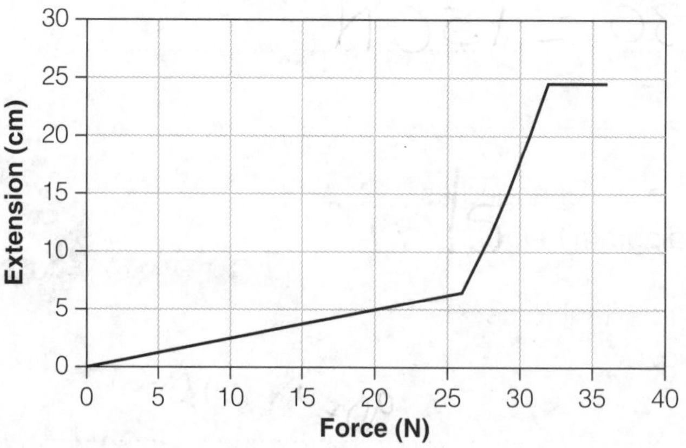

(i) What term is given to the relationship shown in this graph? (1)

Non-linear

(ii) Explain the difference in the shapes of the two graphs. (3)

1 **(a)** Explain why speed is a scalar quantity while velocity is a vector quantity. (2)

It does not unvolve direction

(b) Draw lines to match the following average speeds to the methods of travel. (4)

Average speed	Travel method
1.5 m/s	Car
6 m/s	Plane
20 m/s	Bicycle
250 m/s	Walking

2 **(a)** A jet ski travels 180 metres in 13 seconds.
What is its speed? (2)

$\frac{D}{S \times t}$

180 ÷ 13 = 13.84

(b) How long would it take for the same jet ski travelling at the same speed to travel 500 m? (2)

~~500 ÷ 13.84 = 36.12 min~~

36.12 sec

Speed and velocity

Module 67

D / S × T

1 The graph shows the distance a boat travels over time.

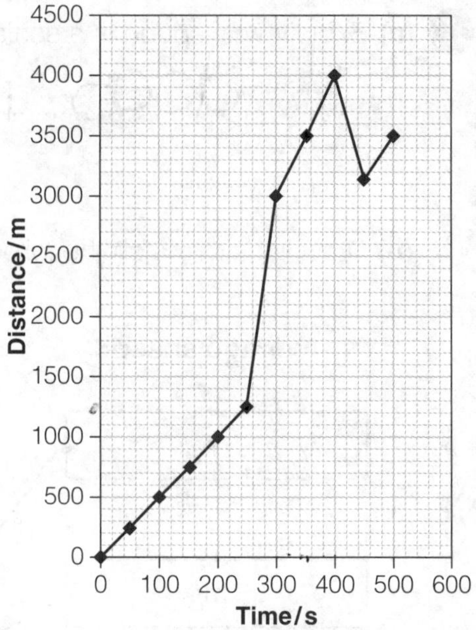

(a) What is the average speed of the boat over the first 350 seconds? (2)

D / T

3500 ÷ 350 = 10

(b) What is the velocity of the boat at 265 seconds? (2)

1250 ÷ 265 = 4.716

2 The graph shows the velocity of a car.

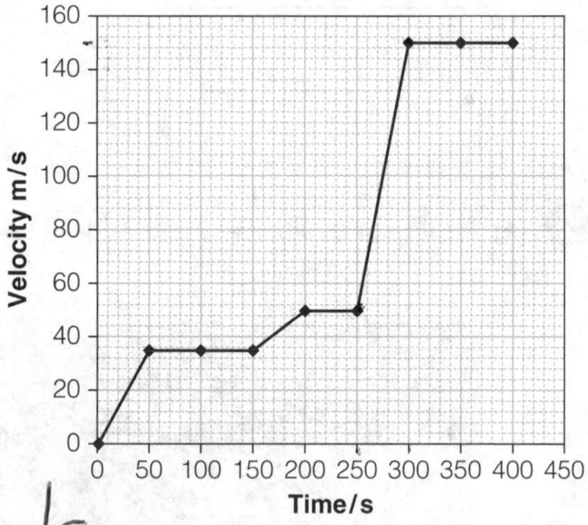

(a) During what time period is the greatest acceleration of the car? (1)

250 to 300

(b) What is the acceleration during this time period? (2)

150 ÷ 250 = 0.6 m/s

3 Explain why a skydiver in free fall accelerates for a time before maintaining a constant speed. (4)

Force of Gravity.

1 **(a)** What will happen if a resultant force greater than zero is applied to:

(i) a stationary object? (1)

....

(ii) a moving object? (1)

....

(b) Which of Newton's laws deals with the effect of resultant force? (1)

....

2 **(a)** The acceleration of an object is inversely proportional to the mass of an object. How does the acceleration relate to the resultant force? (1)

....

(b) **(i)** Adele, a cyclist, who has a total mass of 110 kg, accelerates at 5 m/s^2. What is the resultant force on Adele? (2)

....

....

(ii) Explain how the resultant force on Adele will change as she slows down and comes to a stop. (3)

....

....

....

3 State Newton's third law. (1)

....

4 Use Newton's laws to explain the events that the sign below is warning about. (3)

....

....

....

....

1 (a) Increasing speed increases the thinking distance and the braking distance of a car. Explain why. (2)

(i) Thinking distance:

A faster vehicle travels further during time taken to react.

(ii) Braking distance:

Car will travel further in time taken for driver to put on the breaks

(b) Give **two** other factors that could increase the thinking distance. (2)

tiredness

Alcohol

(c) The table shows the temperatures of brakes when a car decelerates to zero in a set amount of time.

The test was repeated at four different initial speeds.

Test	Brake temperature (°C)
A	150
B	800
C	320
D	560

(i) Put the tests in order of initial speed, from highest speed to lowest speed. (1)

B, D, C, A

(ii) Explain your answer. (2)

(iii) How would the results change if the experiment was repeated with all the variables the same except the car decelerating in a shorter amount of time? (2)

Forces and braking

Module 70

1 Jessica, a sky diver, is in a plane at a height of 3900 m. She has a mass of 60 kg.

(a) What is Jessica's gravitational potential energy?

(Assume gravitational field strength is 10 N/kg.) (2)

2,340,000 kJ

(b) Jessica jumps from the plane and accelerates to a terminal velocity of 55 m/s. What is Jessica's kinetic energy at this point? (2)

90,750 J

(c) Jessica deploys her parachute and slows to a speed of 5 m/s. What is her new kinetic energy? (2)

750 J

(d) When Jessica lands on the ground, she is stationary. What is her kinetic energy now? (1)

0 J

2 The table below shows the specific heat capacity of different substances.

Substance	Specific heat capacity J/kg/°C
Water	4180
Copper	390
Ethanol	2440
Titanium	520

(a) Which substance would require the least energy to raise 1 kg by 1°C? Explain how you arrived at your answer. (2)

(b) Calculate the mass of copper that requires 76 kJ of energy to increase in temperature from 16°C to 35°C. (3)

Changes in energy

Module 71

1 Which of the below is an incorrect ending to the following sentence?
Tick the correct options. (2)

Energy cannot be...

- created. ☐
- transferred. ☑
- destroyed. ☐
- dissipated. ☑

2 The table below shows the average cost of heating three different houses.
Each home is the same size.

House	Heating cost per hour / p
A	105
B	88
C	150

(a) Which house is likely to have the best insulation in its walls?
Explain how you arrived at your answer. (3)

B. ~~less gets out~~

(b) Can you be certain about your conclusion?
Explain your answer. (3)

(c) The boiler in another house is 65% efficient. If the energy input is 5400 kJ, what is the useful energy output? (2)

1. Complete the table below to give **three** examples of renewable energy and **three** examples of non-renewable energy. (3)

Renewable energy	Non-renewable energy
Bio-fuel	Nuclear fuel
Wind	Oil
Solar Power	Coal

2. The graph below shows the percentage of the total electricity in the UK generated by wind turbines.

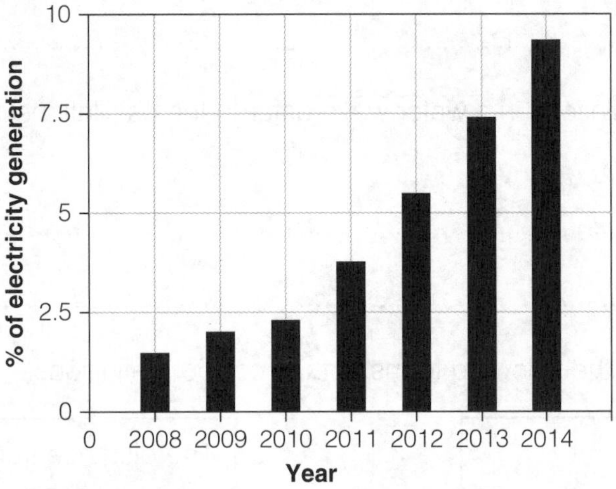

(a) Describe the trend shown by the graph. (1)

more where being placed.

(b) Describe the main advantage of wind power over burning fossil fuels. (2)

its a renewable resource

(c) Will wind turbines ever make up 100% of electricity generation? Explain your answer. (3)

No because its not always reliable.

(d) Why might some people not want wind turbines to be placed on the tops of hills? (1)

They say there ugly and would ruin Landscape

National and global energy resources

Module 73

1 The speed of sound in water is 1482 m/s.

(a) What type of wave is a sound wave when travelling in air? (1)

Longitudinal waves.

(b) Calculate the wavelength of a sound wave in water that has a frequency of 120 Hz. (2)

$\frac{1482}{120} = 12.35.$

(c) The speed of sound in air is 330 m/s.
Suggest a reason for the difference between this speed and the speed of sound in water. (2)

(d) How do the oscillations in a water wave differ to the oscillations in a sound wave travelling in air? (2)

2 Draw lines to match the following terms to their correct definitions. (3)

Amplitude	The distance from a point on one wave to the equivalent point on the adjacent wave.
Wavelength	The number of waves passing a point each second.
Frequency	The maximum displacement of a point on a wave away from its undisturbed position.

(Lines drawn: Amplitude — The maximum displacement of a point on a wave away from its undisturbed position; Wavelength — The distance from a point on one wave to the equivalent point on the adjacent wave; Frequency — The number of waves passing a point each second.)

1 The image below shows the electromagnetic spectrum.

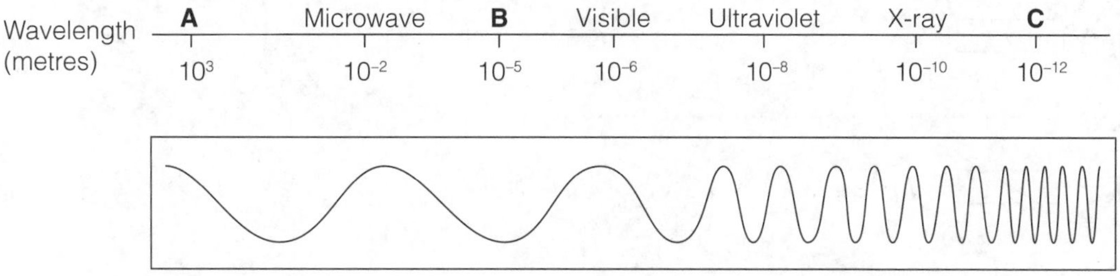

What are the names of the different types of electromagnetic radiation **A**–**C**? (3)

A: ....

B: ....

C: ....

2 **(a)** From where do gamma rays originate? (1)

....

(b) Give **one** potential use of gamma rays. (1)

treatment of cancer

(c) Why are gamma rays potentially harmful? (2)

They can have hazardous effects on body tissue.

3 What variable could be measured to determine the possible harm caused by radiation? (1)

....

4 Both visible light and X-rays are used by astronomers to observe the Universe. The speed of light in space is 299792458 m/s.

What is the speed of X-rays?

Explain how you arrived at your answer. (3)

....

....

....

1 Identify the following circuit symbols:

(a) 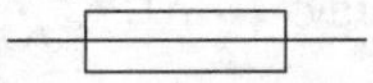 (1)

....

(b) 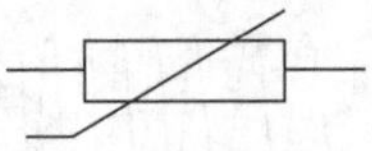 (1)

....

(c)  (1)

....

2 The diagram shows a circuit.

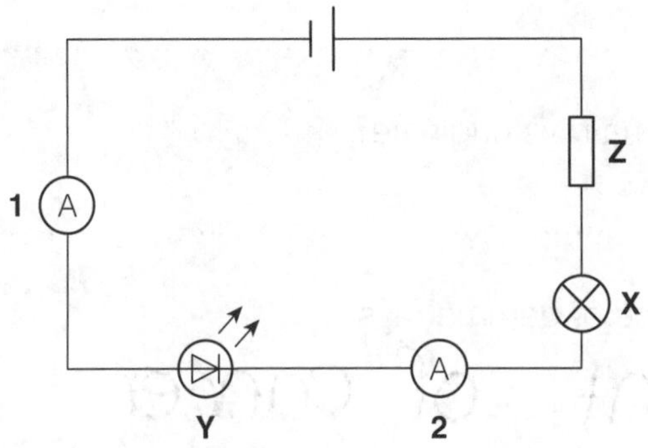

(a) Identify components **X**, **Y** and **Z**. (3)

X: ....

Y: ....

Z: ....

(b) Ammeter **1** gave a reading of 5 amps.
What is the reading of ammeter **2**? (1)

....

(c) What is 'electric current'? (1)

....

(d) If the charge flow through the circuit was 780 C, for how long was the current flowing through the circuit? (2)

....

....

1 The graph shows the relationship between the current and potential difference of a component.

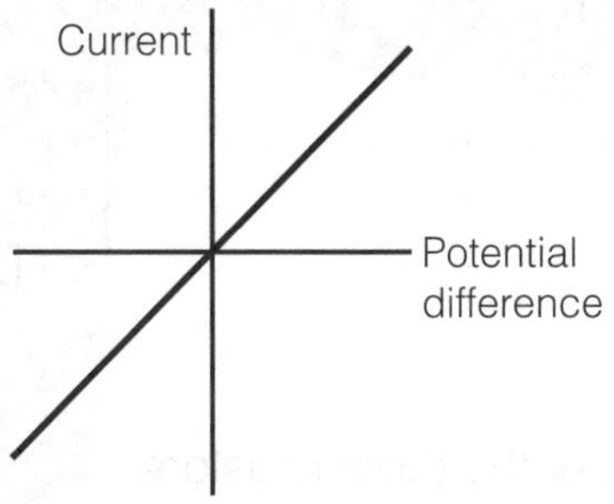

(a) What general name could be given to this type of conductor? (1)

....

(b) What environmental factor could change and lead to a change in the shape of the graph above? (1)

....

(c) On the axis, sketch a graph to show the relationship between current and potential difference through a diode. (2)

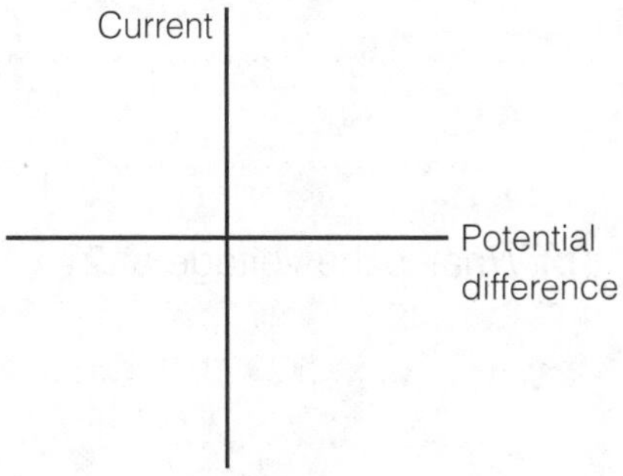

2 Calculate the current flowing through a 4 Ω resistor when there is a potential difference of 15 V across it. (2)

....

....

3 Look at the circuit below.

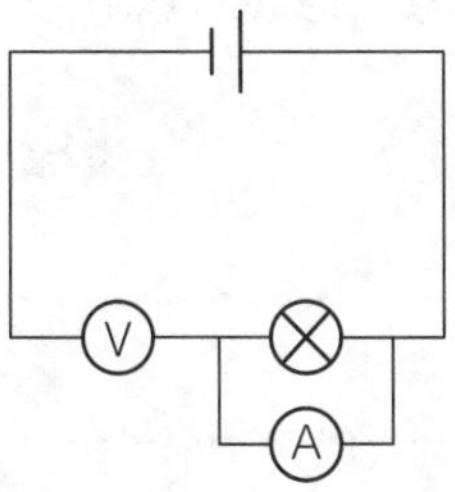

Explain why this circuit could not be used to determine the resistance of the lamp. (3)

....

....

....

Module 78

Series and parallel circuits

1 The diagram shows a circuit.

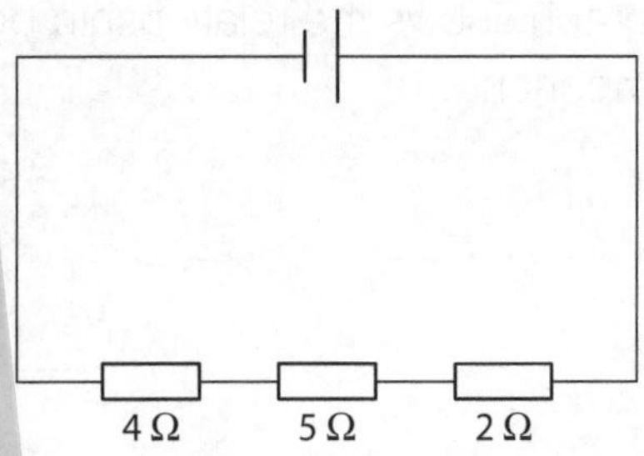

(a) What type of circuit is shown? (1)

....

....

(b) What is the total resistance of the three resistors in the circuit? Show how you arrived at your answer. (2)

....

....

2 The diagram shows a circuit.

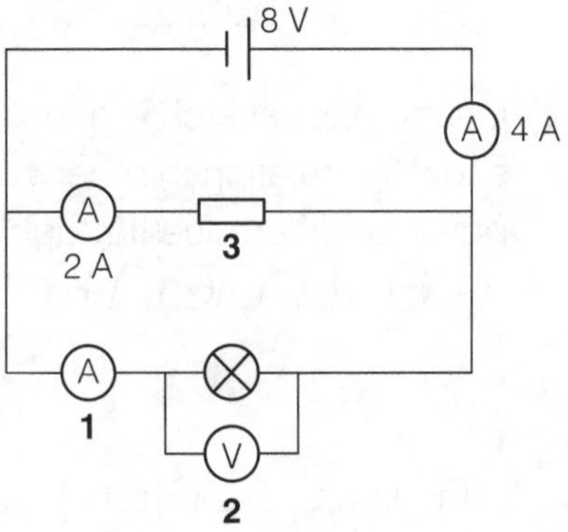

(a) What is the current at **1**? (1)

....

....

(b) What is the voltage at **2**? (1)

....

....

(c) What is the resistance at **3**? (1)

....

....

(d) The circuit was rewired so that the lamp and resistor were wired in series. How would this change the total resistance of the two components?

Explain your answer. (3)

....

....

....

1 Draw lines to match the names of the wires in a plug to its colour and function. (3)

Wire	Colour	Function
Live wire	Blue	Completes the circuit.
Neutral wire	Brown	Only carries a current if there is a fault.
Earth wire	Green and yellow stripes	Carries the alternating potential difference from the supply.

2 An electric sander is being used during a house renovation. The sander is plugged into a socket in the wall.

(a) Is the sander powered by direct current or alternating current?

Explain your answer. (2)

....

....

(b) Fully explain why it would be dangerous to operate the sander if the wire became damaged. (4)

....

....

....

....

(c) Explain why this risk would be decreased if the sander was powered by two 1.5V batteries. (2)

....

....

1 **(a)** A tumble dryer has a current flowing through it of 3 A and a resistance of 76.7 Ω.

Calculate its power. (2)

(b) What useful energy transfers are occurring in the tumble dryer? (2)

(c) If the tumble dryer transfers 180 kJ of energy in a cycle, how long is the cycle in seconds? (2)

(d) The mains electricity used by the tumble dryer has a potential difference of 230 V. Some of the overhead cables that carry the electricity in the National Grid have a potential difference of 138 kV.

Explain the reasons for this difference in potential difference. (3)

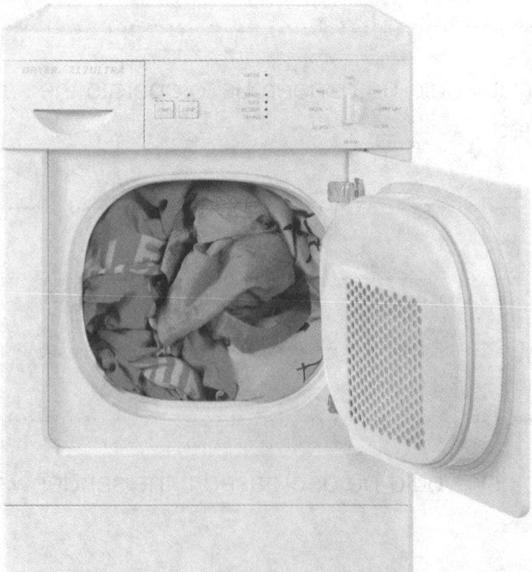

1 Complete the diagram below to show the poles of the three bar magnets interacting. (3)

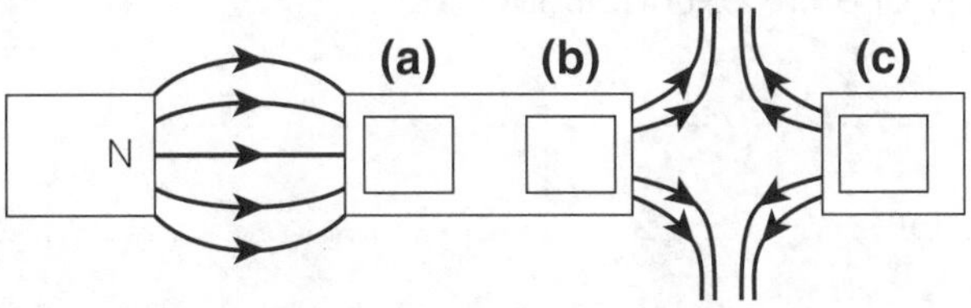

2 The diagram below shows an experiment into magnets and magnetic objects.

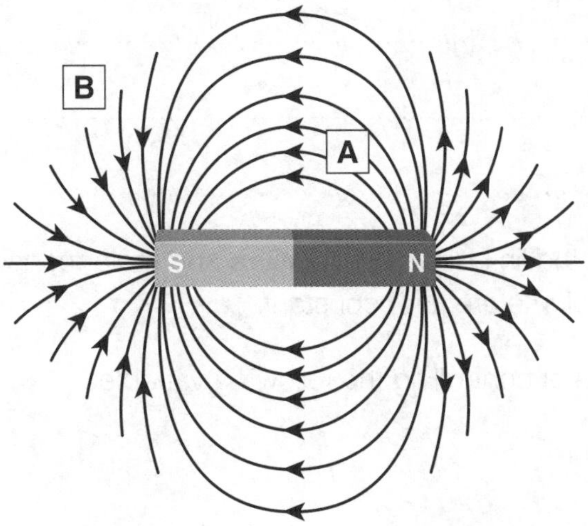

(a) What name is given to the region around the magnet where magnetic objects or magnets experience a force? (1)

....

(b) What type of force would a magnetic object placed at **A** experience? (1)

....

(c) Would the force at **A** be stronger than the force experienced by a magnetic object at **B**? Explain your answer. (2)

....

....

3 Tick each of the following statements that correctly describe the features of a solenoid. (2)

The magnetic field around a solenoid is the same shape as the magnetic field around a bar magnet.	☐
Adding an iron core to a solenoid reduces the magnetic strength of the solenoid.	☐
A solenoid with an iron core is an electromagnet.	☐
A solenoid with a tin core is an electromagnet	☐
A solenoid is a non-conducting wire formed into a helix.	☐

1 **(a)** A full fire extinguisher has a mass of 5 kg and a volume of 0.002 m^3. What is the density of a fire extinguisher? (2)

....

....

(b) What would happen to the density of the fire extinguisher after it had been used to put out a fire? Explain your answer. (3)

....

....

....

2 In an investigation into the link between pressure and molar concentration of a gas, the temperature and volume are kept constant.

Explain the importance of controlling the following variables:

(a) Constant temperature (1)

....

(b) Constant volume (1)

....

3 **(a)** What mass of water is produced by heating 3 kg of ice until it has completely melted? Explain how you arrived at your answer. (2)

....

....

(b) The temperature of the water is then lowered past its freezing point and ice reforms. How does this prove that the original melting was a physical change as opposed to a chemical change? (2)

....

....

....

1 The graph below shows the results of an investigation into the heating of a substance.

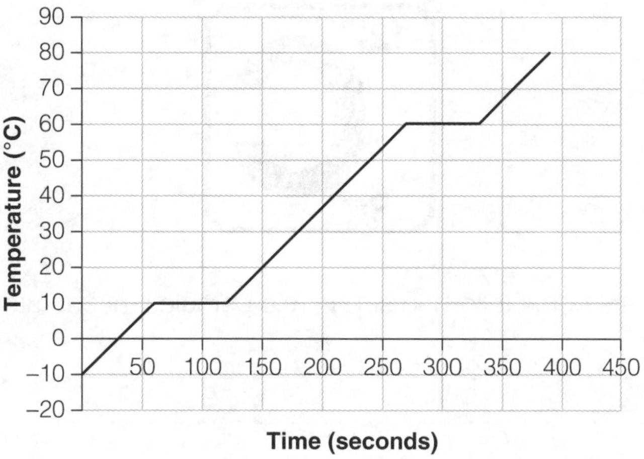

(a) At what temperatures did the substance do the following?

(i) Melt:

.... (1)

(ii) Boil:

.... (1)

(b) Explain how you arrived at your answers for part **(a)**. (3)

....

....

....

(c) The substance has a specific latent heat of melting of 250 kJ/kg.

What is the energy required to melt 500 g of the substance? (2)

....

....

1 An element symbol is shown below.

$$^{12}_{6}\mathrm{C}$$

(a) State the numbers of the following subatomic particles that an atom of the element contains.

(i) Protons: .... (1)

(ii) Neutrons: .... (1)

(iii) Electrons: .... (1)

(b) The element is also found in the following forms:

$^{12}\mathrm{C}$ $^{13}\mathrm{C}$ $^{14}\mathrm{C}$

(i) What name is given to these forms? (1)

....

(ii) How do they differ from each other? (1)

....

2 **(a)** Give **two** differences between the plum pudding model of atomic structure and Rutherford, Geiger and Marsden's nuclear model. (2)

....

....

(b) Why was James Chadwick's experimental work in 1932 important in further developing the model of atomic structure? (1)

....

1 An investigation was carried out into the penetration of radiation emitted from different radioactive sources.

Type of radiation	Radiation released	Penetration distance in air
A	Two neutrons and two protons (a helium nucleus).	A few centimetres.
B	Electromagnetic radiation from the nucleus.	A large distance.
C	High speed electron ejected from the nucleus as a neutron turns into a proton.	A few metres.

(a) (i) Identify the types of radiation **A**–**C**. (3)

A: ....

B: ....

C: ....

(ii) Rank the radiations in **(i)** from most ionising to least ionising. (2)

....

Most ionising **Least ionising**

2 The equation below shows the decay of a radioactive element.

$$^{238}_{\mathbf{A}}U \longrightarrow {}^{\mathbf{B}}_{90}Th + {}^{\mathbf{C}}_{\mathbf{D}}\alpha$$

(a) What type of decay is shown by the equation? (1)

....

(b) Complete the missing parts (**A**–**D**) of the equation. (3)

A: ....

B: ....

C: ....

D: ....

(c) What effect does gamma emission have on the nucleus of a radioactive element? (1)

....

....

1 Complete the following paragraph using some of the words below. (3)

decay	**irradiation**	**Sievert**	**contamination**
radioactive	**half-life**	**emit**	**radiation**

Radioactive .... is the unwanted presence of materials containing radioactive atoms on other materials. This is a hazard due to the .... of the contaminating atoms. The atoms will .... radiation so may be a hazard. .... is the process of exposing an object to nuclear .... without the object itself becoming ....

2 The graph below shows the decay of a radioactive element.

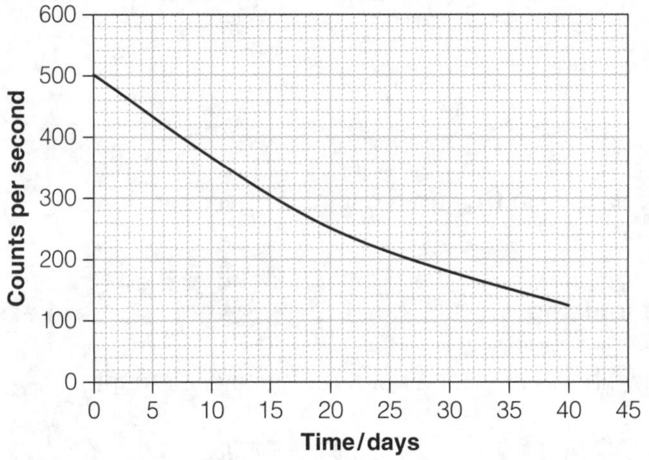

(a) (i) Estimate the half-life of this element. (1)

....

(ii) Explain how you arrived at your answer. (1)

....

(iii) Estimate the counts per second of the sample after 60 days. (2)

....

....

Notes

Letts

F

GCSE

COMBINED SCIENCE: TRILOGY

Foundation Tier   Paper 1: Biology 1F

Time allowed: 1 hour 15 minutes

You may use:

- a ruler
- a calculator

Instructions

- Answer **all** questions in the spaces provided.
- Do all rough work in this book. Cross through any work you do not want to be marked.

Information

- There are 70 marks available on this paper.
- The marks for questions are shown in brackets.
- You are expected to use a calculator where appropriate.
- You are reminded of the need for good English and clear presentation in your answers.
- When answering question 08.3 you need to make sure that your answer:
  - is clear, logical, sensibly structured
  - fully meets the requirements of the question
  - shows that each separate point or step supports the overall answer.

Advice

- In all calculations, show clearly how you work out your answer.

Name: ____________________

0 1 This question is about plants.

0 1 . 1 Which of the following structures are in the correct size order, starting with the smallest?
Tick (✓) **one** box. **[1 mark]**

cell, tissue, organ, system ☐

tissue, organ, system, cell ☐

cell, organ, system, tissue ☐

tissue, system, cell, organ ☐

0 1 . 2 Which substance is a product of aerobic respiration in plants? Tick (✓) **one** box. **[1 mark]**

Carbon dioxide ☐

Ethanol ☐

Glucose ☐

Lactic acid ☐

0 1 . 3 Plants and animals use glucose for respiration. Plants also convert glucose in to different substances.

Draw a line to match the new substance to why plants need it. **[2 marks]**

Starch	To make cell walls
Cellulose	For protein synthesis
Amino acids	For storage

0 1 . 4 Plants need energy for living processes. Where does this energy come from? **[2 marks]**

____

____

0 2 **Figure 1** shows an image of an onion cell taken using a microscope with a 10× eyepiece and a 40× objective lens.

Figure 1

A ____________

B ____________

C ____________

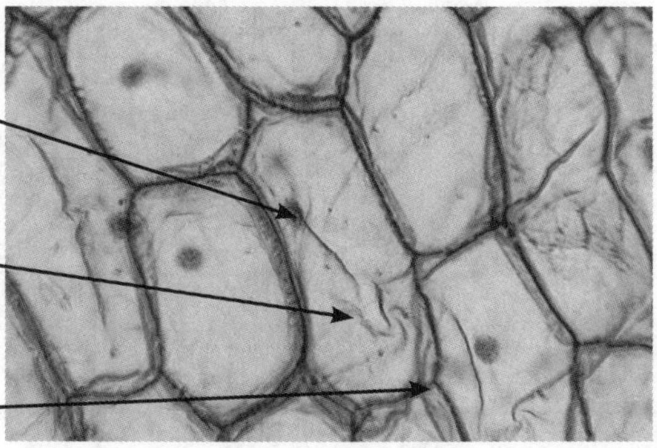

0 2 . 1 Label **Figure 1** using three of the words in the box below. **[3 marks]**

cell membrane chloroplast nucleus cell wall cytoplasm vacuole chromosome

0 2 . 2 Which of the following is found in a plant cell but not in an animal cell?
Tick (✓) **one** box. **[1 mark]**

Cell membrane ☐

Cytoplasm ☐

Nucleus ☐

Cell wall ☐

0 2 . 3 What is the total magnification of the onion cell in **Figure 1**? Tick (✓) **one** box. **[1 mark]**

×40 ☐

×50 ☐

×100 ☐

×400 ☐

0 2 . 4 An electron microscope has a much higher magnification than microscopes used in the school laboratory.

Explain how electron microscopy has increased our understanding of the structure of cells.
[2 marks]

____

____

0 3 This question is about respiration,

0 3 . 1 Which substance is a product of anaerobic respiration in humans? Tick (✓) **one** box. **[1 mark]**

Carbon dioxide ☐

Ethanol ☐

Glucose ☐

Lactic acid ☐

0 3 . 2

Figure 2

Niamh in **Figure 2** is training for a marathon. Every few days she runs a long distance. This builds up the number of mitochondria in her muscle cells.

What is the advantage for Niamh of having extra mitochondria in her muscle cells?
Tick (✓) **one** box. **[1 mark]**

Her muscles become stronger. ☐

Her muscles can contract faster. ☐

Her muscles can release more energy. ☐

Her muscles can repair faster after injury. ☐

0 3 . 3 Bob in **Figure 3** has been running hard and has an oxygen debt. Describe what causes an oxygen debt after a session of vigorous exercise and how Bob can recover from its effects.

[3 marks]

Figure 3

____

____

____

____

0 3 . 4 Tariq is competing in a 10-mile running race. His heart rate and breathing rate increase. Describe how this helps his muscles during the race. **[3 marks]**

____

____

____

0 4 **Figure 4** shows a diagram of the heart.

Figure 4

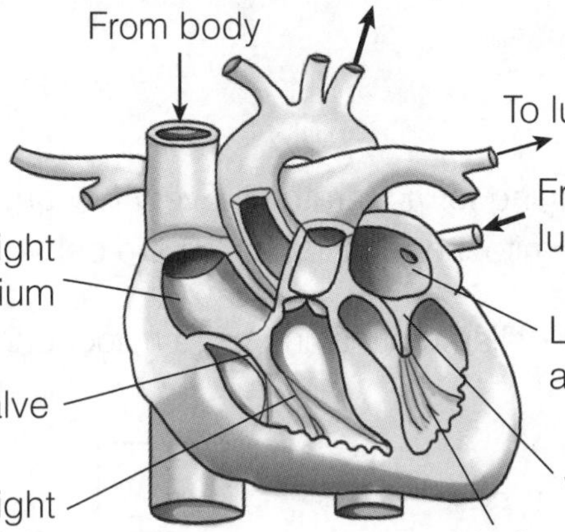

0 4 . 1 Draw arrows on the diagram to show how the blood flows from the heart to the lungs. **[1 mark]**

0 4 . 2 Explain why the left side of the heart is more muscular than the right side. **[1 mark]**

____

____

0 4 . 3 The heart contains a number of valves.

Describe how the valves help the heart pump blood more effectively. **[1 mark]**

____

____

0 4 . 4 There are around 105 650 deaths in the UK from smoking-related causes each year. The number of deaths due to cardiovascular disease that is linked to smoking is estimated to be 22 100.

What percentage of deaths from smoking each year is due to cardiovascular disease? Show your working. Give your answer to two significant figures. **[2 marks]**

____

0 4 . 5 The chance of heart disease can be reduced by lowering alcohol intake and by not smoking. Write about **two** other choices that can be made to reduce the chance of heart disease.

[2 marks]

____

____

0 5 **Figure 5** shows an experiment to investigate how water is taken up by a plant.

Figure 5

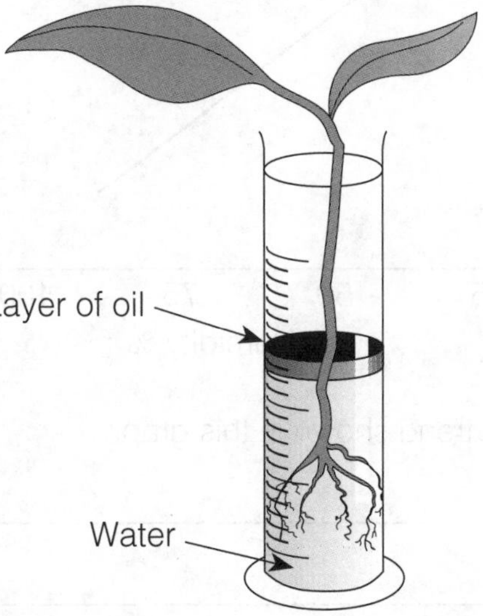

0 5 . 1 What is the purpose of the layer of oil? **[1 mark]**

____

0 5 . 2 **Table 1** shows the results of the experiment.

Table 1

Time (days)	0	1	2	3	4
Volume of water in cylinder (cm^3)	50	47	43	42	40

Calculate the average water loss per day from the measuring cylinder in **Figure 5**.
Show your working. **[2 marks]**

____

____

Average water loss: ____________ cm^3 per day

0 5 . 3 Explain why plants need water. **[2 marks]**

____

____

0 5 . 4 Not all of the water is used by the plant. Describe how water is lost by transpiration. **[2 marks]**

____

____

0 5 . 5 The graph in **Figure 6** shows the relationship between humidity and the rate of transpiration.

Figure 6

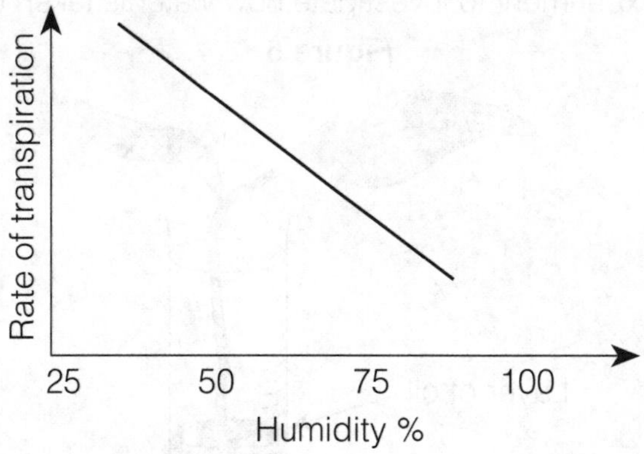

Describe and explain the trend shown in this graph. **[3 marks]**

____

____

____

0 6 This question is about enzymes.

0 6 . 1 Which of the following substances breaks down starch during digestion?
Tick (✓) **one** box. **[1 mark]**

Amylase ☐

Cellulose ☐

Lipase ☐

Protease ☐

0 6 . 2 Which of the following substances breaks down protein during digestion?
Tick (✓) **one** box. **[1 mark]**

Glycerol ☐

Amino acids ☐

Protease ☐

Lipase ☐

0 6 . 3 A group of students were investigating how different reaction conditions affect enzyme activity. They used an enzyme that catalyses the breakdown of protein. The results of the experiment are shown in **Table 2**.

Table 2

pH	1	2	3	4	5
Rate of reaction (mg per minute)	10.5	23.0	10.0	2.5	0.0

Draw a graph showing these results. **[3 marks]**

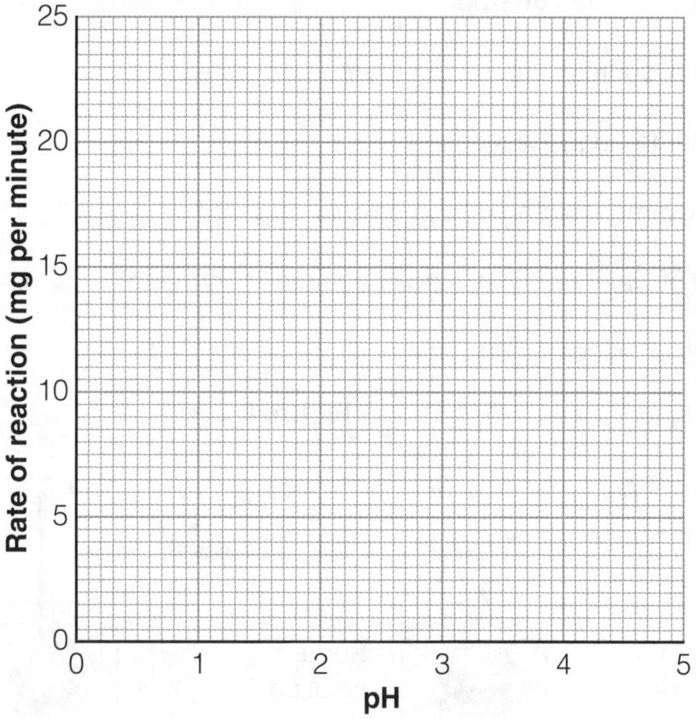

0 6 . 4 Explain the shape of the graph. **[3 marks]**

____

____

____

0 6 . 5 A new pH-controlled biological washing powder (see **Figure 7**) contains protease and lipase enzymes. It is very good at removing food stains from clothing in a 30 °C wash.

Figure 7

Why is the washing powder pH controlled? **[1 mark]**

____

0 6 . 6 Explain why the washing powder is less effective when used in a 60 °C wash. **[2 marks]**

____

____

0 7 This question is about osmosis.

0 7 . 1 What is osmosis? Tick (✓) **one** box. **[1 mark]**

The movement of sucrose around the plant ☐

The loss of water through the stomata ☐

The random movement of particles in a liquid or gas ☐

The movement of water particles across a partially permeable membrane ☐

0 7 . 2 **Figure 8** shows an experiment to demonstrate osmosis.

Figure 8

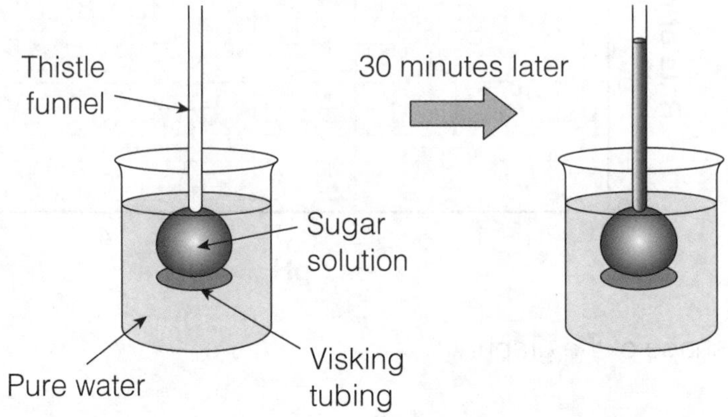

Explain why the volume of solution inside the thistle funnel has increased. **[3 marks]**

____

____

____

0 8 This question is about photosynthesis.

0 8 . 1 Thomas burns paraffin in a small stove inside his greenhouse during March and April. How does this benefit the growth of his greenhouse plants? **[2 marks]**

____

____

0 8 . 2 Complete the word equation for photosynthesis.

Carbon dioxide + ______________ $\xrightarrow[\text{chlorophyll}]{\text{sunlight}}$ glucose + ______________

[2 marks]

0 8 . 3 Anoushka investigates the effect of light on photosynthesis at 25 °C.
She uses the apparatus shown in **Figure 9**.

Figure 9

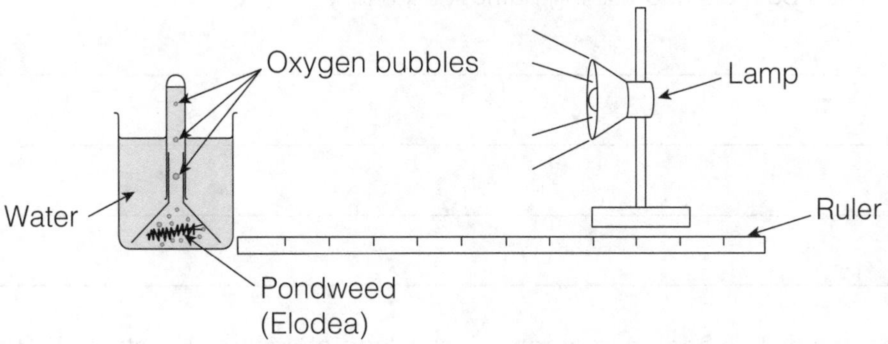

She moves the lamp and counts the bubbles at different distances from the pondweed. **Table 3** shows her results.

Table 3

Distance from lamp to pondweed (cm)	Number of bubbles counted in five minutes
10	241
20	124
30	60
40	36
50	24

Describe the pattern in the results in **Table 3** and predict how the pattern would change if the experiment was repeated at 35 °C and at 55 °C. Explain your answers. **[6 marks]**

0 9 This question is about aseptic technique.

0 9 . 1 Describe the aseptic method used to grow a colony of bacteria cells from pond water using a sterilised petri dish containing nutrient agar jelly. **[4 marks]**

____

____

____

____

0 9 . 2 After the culture had been prepared, one drop of each disinfectant, A, B and C was added to the culture. The petri dish incubated for three days.

Look at **Figure 10**.

Figure 10

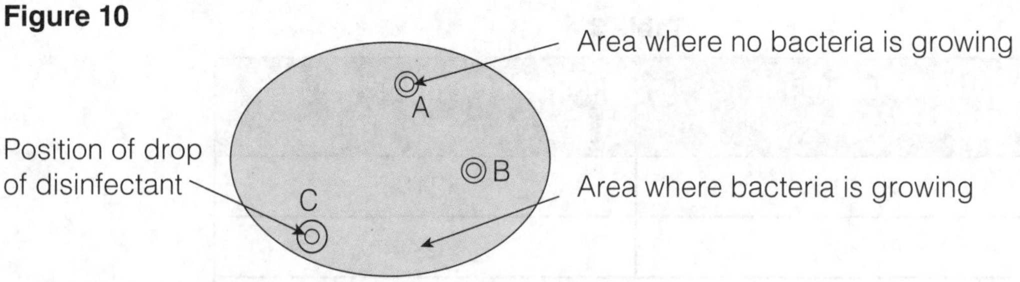

State which disinfectant you would use to clean the surface after the pond water had been spilt on it. Give reasons for your answer. **[3 marks]**

____

____

____

END OF QUESTIONS

Letts

F

GCSE

COMBINED SCIENCE: TRILOGY

Foundation Tier   Paper 2: Biology 2F

Time allowed: 1 hour 15 minutes

You may use:

- a ruler
- a calculator

Instructions

- Answer **all** questions in the spaces provided.
- Do all rough work in this book. Cross through any work you do not want to be marked.

Information

- There are 70 marks available on this paper.
- The marks for questions are shown in brackets.
- You are expected to use a calculator where appropriate.
- You are reminded of the need for good English and clear presentation in your answers.
- When answering question 10.1 you need to make sure that your answer:
  - is clear, logical, sensibly structured
  - fully meets the requirements of the question
  - shows that each separate point or step supports the overall answer.

Advice

- In all calculations, show clearly how you work out your answer.

Name: ______________________________

0 1 **Figure 1** shows a simple food chain. The arrows represent the transfer of energy in the food chain.

Figure 1

0 1 . 1 Which word describes the grass? Tick (✓) **one** box. **[1 mark]**

Producer ☐

Consumer ☐

Predator ☐

Prey ☐

0 1 . 2 Which word describes the fox? Tick (✓) **one** box. **[1 mark]**

Producer ☐

Consumer ☐

Predator ☐

Prey ☐

0 1 . 3 Fifty years ago, there was an outbreak of myxomatosis that killed nearly all the rabbits.

What do you think happened to the stoat population? Give a reason for your answer. **[2 marks]**

____

____

0 1 . 4 In **Figure 1**, which arrow shows the greatest transfer of energy? Tick (✓) **one** box. **[1 mark]**

A ☐

B ☐

C ☐

D ☐

0 2 **Figure 2** shows a tree grown on its own. **Figure 3** shows trees in a forest.

Figure 2

Figure 3

0 2 . 1 Write down two differences between the trees in **Figure 2** and **Figure 3**. **[2 marks]**

____

____

____

0 2 . 2 The trees in the forest have to compete with each other for things they need to grow.

Name **two** abiotic factors that the tree must compete for. **[2 marks]**

____

____

0 2 . 3 Ella wants to compare the number and types of plant found growing by the single tree with those growing in the forest. In her investigation she uses a quadrat.
What is a quadrat? **[1 mark]**

____

0 2 . 4 Ella places the quadrat near the single tree. **Figure 4** shows the results.

Figure 4

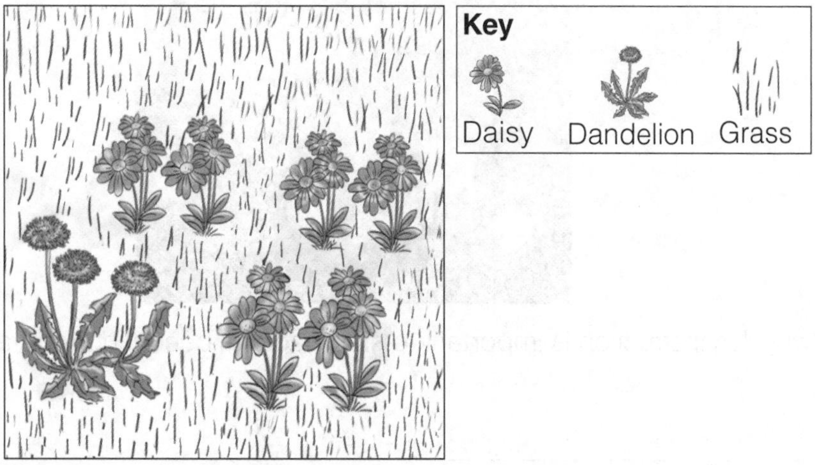

How many different types of plant are growing in the area? **[1 mark]**

____

0 2 . 5 Estimate the percentage cover of grass. **[1 mark]**

___

0 2 . 6 Next, Ella takes the quadrat into the forest to get more results. What do you think will happen to the percentage cover of grass? Give a reason for your answer. **[2 marks]**

___

___

0 2 . 7 Explain how Ella's investigation could be improved. **[4 marks]**

___

___

___

___

0 3 This question is about antibiotics.

0 3 . 1 What types of disease are antibiotics used to treat? Tick (✓) **one** box. **[1 mark]**

Bacterial ☐

Fungal ☐

Viral ☐

Hereditary ☐

0 3 . 2 The following text is one of the instructions on a packet of antibiotic tablets (see **Figure 5**):
Complete the prescribed course of treatment as directed by your doctor.

Figure 5

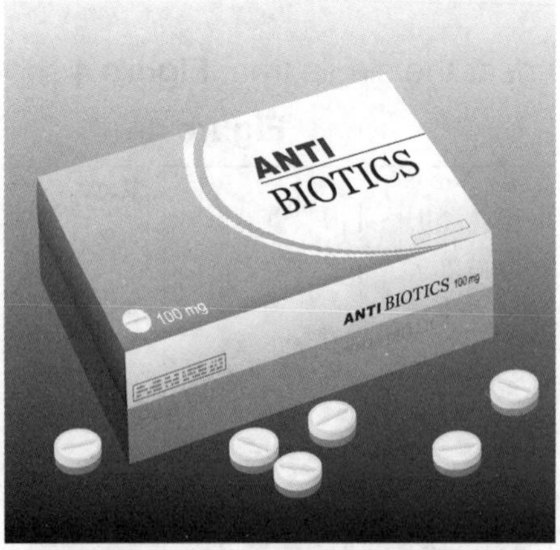

Explain why this instruction is important to stop bacteria becoming resistant to this antibiotic. **[3 marks]**

___

___

___

0 3 . 3 Describe two measures that can be taken to stop bacteria from becoming resistant to antibiotics.

[2 marks]

____

____

0 4 **Figure 6** shows a fossil.

Figure 6

0 4 . 1 What living thing does the fossil look like? **[1 mark]**

____

0 4 . 2 What is a fossil? **[1 mark]**

____

____

0 4 . 3 Why are fossils only found in sedimentary rocks? **[1 mark]**

____

____

0 4 . 4 What can scientists learn from fossils? **[2 marks]**

____

____

0 5 Two students carried out an experiment to investigate the decay of grass cuttings.

- They put the cuttings in three different-coloured plastic bags – each bag had a few very small holes for ventilation.
- The bags were placed together at the edge of the school field.
- The bags were weighed at the start of the experiment and again three months later.

Table 1 shows the results.

Table 1

	Black bag (A)	Yellow bag (B)	White bag (C)
Mass of bag and grass cuttings at the start (g)	320.4	350.6	325.7
Mass of bag and grass cuttings after three months (g)	271.7	305.7	290.9
% decrease in mass	15.2	12.8	10.7

0 5 . 1 Predict the percentage decrease in mass if the experiment is repeated with a dark brown bag. Explain your answer. **[3 marks]**

____

____

____

0 5 . 2 Putting the three bags in the same place on the school field is controlling a variable. Suggest **two** other control variables to help improve this experiment. **[2 marks]**

1. ______________________________

2. ______________________________

0 6 **Figure 7** shows some of the endocrine system.

Figure 7

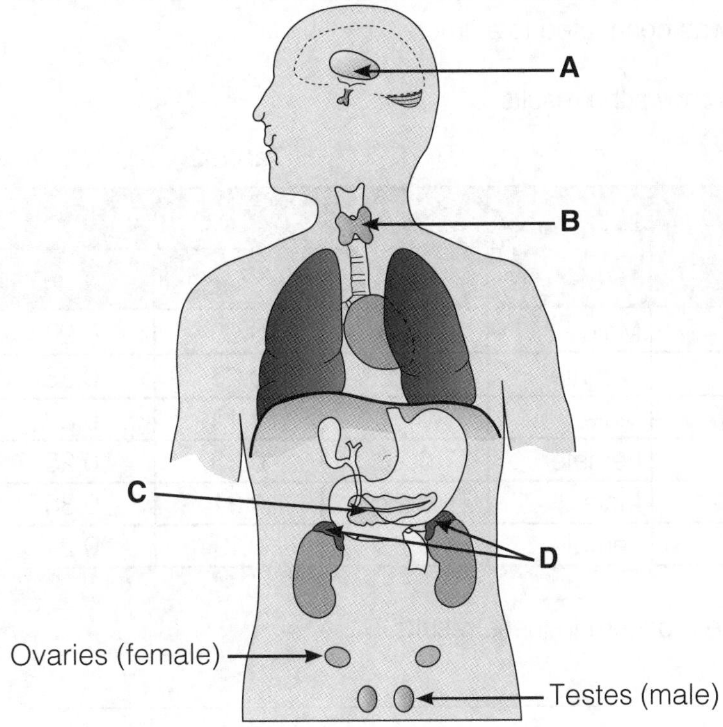

0 6 . 1 Which label shows the adrenal gland?
Tick (✓) **one** box. **[1 mark]**

A ☐

B ☐

C ☐

D ☐

0 6 . 2 Which label shows the thyroid gland? **[1 mark]**
Tick (✓) **one** box.

A ☐

B ☐

C ☐

D ☐

0 6 . 3 Explain why the pituitary gland is sometimes referred to as the 'master gland'. **[3 marks]**

____

____

____

0 7 The reaction times of six people were measured.

They put on headphones and were asked to push a button when they heard a sound. The button was connected to a timer.

Table 2 shows the results.

Table 2

Person	Gender	Reaction time in seconds				
		1	2	3	4	5
A	Male	0.26	0.25	0.27	0.25	0.27
B	Female	0.25	0.25	0.26	0.22	0.24
C	Male	0.31	1.43	0.32	0.29	0.32
D	Female	0.22	0.23	0.25	0.22	0.23
E	Male	0.27	0.31	0.30	0.28	0.26
F	Female	0.23	0.19	0.21	0.21	0.22

0 7 . 1 Describe a pattern in these results. **[1 mark]**

____

0 7 . 2 Calculate the mean reaction time for person C, ignoring any outliers. Show your working. **[2 marks]**

____

____

0 7 . 3 When person D was concentrating on the test, someone touched her arm and she jumped. Her response was a reflex action. What are the **two** main features of a reflex action? **[2 marks]**

____

____

0 7 . 4 A reflex action involves a 'message' travelling along a sensory neurone as an electrical impulse. The electrical impulse reaches a junction called a synapse.

Describe what happens at the synapse for the 'message' to continue its journey. **[4 marks]**

____

____

____

____

0 8 **Figure 8** shows a sheepdog puppy. There are 39 pairs of chromosomes in the skin cell of a sheepdog puppy. Two of the chromosomes determine the sex of the puppy.

Figure 8

0 8 . 1 How many chromosomes are there in the sperm cell of a sheepdog? Tick (✓) **one** box. **[1 mark]**

39 ☐

76 ☐

78 ☐

80 ☐

0 8 . 2 The number of skin cells increases as the puppy grows.

After a period of growth, a skin cell divides into two. What is the name of this process? Explain why each skin cell has the same number of chromosomes. **[4 marks]**

____

____

____

____

0 9 This question is about genes.

0 9 . 1 What is selective breeding? **[1 mark]**

____

0 9 . 2 Which term describes different versions of the same gene?
Tick (✓) **one** box. **[1 mark]**

Variant ☐

Dominant ☐

Recessive ☐

Allele ☐

0 9 . 3 You want to breed a plant with red and white flowers. Two alleles control the flower colour: red (R) and white (r). The red allele is dominant.

The genetic cross from the breeding is shown in **Figure 9**.

Figure 9

	R	r
r	Rr	
r		

Complete **Figure 9**. **[2 marks]**

0 9 . 4 On **Figure 9**, circle one of the offspring that has a white flower. **[1 mark]**

0 9 . 5 What is the probability of getting a red flower? **[1 mark]**

____

0 9 . 6 Explain why biodiversity is important. **[3 marks]**

____

____

1 0 Diabetes is a condition where the body cannot control the level of glucose in the blood.

1 0 . 1 Describe how the human body normally controls the level of glucose in the blood and how people with type 1 and type 2 diabetes maintain the correct levels of glucose in the blood. **[6 marks]**

____

____

____

____

____

____

____

____

____

____

10.2 Diabetes can adversely affect the kidneys.

Kidneys remove urea from the bloodstream. Outline what other jobs the kidneys do. **[2 marks]**

END OF QUESTIONS

Letts

F

GCSE

COMBINED SCIENCE: TRILOGY

Foundation Tier Paper 3: Chemistry 1F

Time allowed: 1 hour 15 minutes

You may use:

- a ruler
- a calculator

Instructions

- Answer **all** questions in the spaces provided.
- Do all rough work in this book. Cross through any work you do not want to be marked.

Information

- There are 70 marks available on this paper.
- The marks for questions are shown in brackets.
- You are expected to use a calculator where appropriate.
- You are reminded of the need for good English and clear presentation in your answers.
- When answering question 08.4 you need to make sure that your answer:
  - is clear, logical, sensibly structured
  - fully meets the requirements of the question
  - shows that each separate point or step supports the overall answer.

Advice

- In all calculations, show clearly how you work out your answer.

Name: ______________________________

0 1 This question is about alloys.

0 1 . 1 What is an alloy?

Tick (✓) **one** box. **[1 mark]**

Metal ☐

A mixture of metals ☐

A compound ☐

A mixture ☐

0 1 . 2 Draw a line from the alloy to its most likely use. **[2 marks]**

Alloy	Use
	Statue
Brass	Saxophone
Bronze	Flute
	Waterpipe

0 1 . 3 Steel is an alloy composed mainly of iron.

Explain why steel is a more useful metal than iron. **[2 marks]**

____

____

0 2 The periodic table lists all known elements.

0 2 . 1 Which statement about the periodic table is correct?

Tick (✓) **one** box. **[1 mark]**

Each row begins with elements with one outer electron. ☐

The columns are called periods. ☐

The elements are arranged in mass number order. ☐

The metallic elements are on the right. ☐

0 2 . 2 Which of these statements about the elements in Group 0 is correct?
Tick (✓) **one** box. **[1 mark]**

They are all liquids at room temperature. ☐

Their boiling points increase as you go down the group. ☐

They have very high melting points. ☐

Their molecules are made from pairs of atoms. ☐

0 2 . 3 Element X is a solid with a low melting point. When it reacts it forms covalent bonds with other elements or it forms negative ions.

Put an X where you would expect to find element X on the periodic table. **[1 mark]**

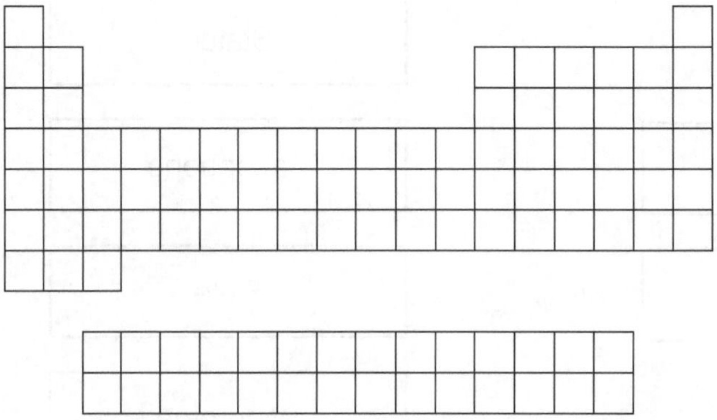

0 2 . 4 Which statement explains why group 1 elements are known as the alkali metals?
Tick (✓) **one** box. **[1 mark]**

They are tested with an alkali to show they are reactive. ☐

They are in the first column in the periodic table. ☐

They all react strongly with alkalis. ☐

They make an alkali when reacted with water. ☐

0 2 . 5 Sodium is below lithium in group 1 of the periodic table.

Explain why sodium reacts more vigorously with water than lithium. **[2 marks]**

____

____

0 3 Acids react with bases to form a salt and water.

Thomas wanted to make a sample of copper sulfate. He started with sulfuric acid and copper oxide.

03.1 The reaction that took place can be written as a symbol equation:

$H_2SO_4(aq) + CuO(s) \rightarrow CuSO_4(aq) + H_2O(l)$

What did the following symbols tell Thomas about the reactants and the products?

aq: ______________________________

s: ______________________________

l: ______________________________ **[4 marks]**

03.2 What type of reaction was Thomas carrying out? Tick (✓) **one** box. **[1 mark]**

- Oxidation ☐
- Reduction ☐
- Neutralisation ☐
- Decomposition ☐

03.3 Thomas put the sulfuric acid into a beaker and measured the pH. He then added the copper oxide and gently warmed the beaker. When the colourless solution turned blue, he measured the pH again.

What safety precautions should Thomas take when carrying out the practical? **[2 marks]**

____

____

03.4 Which ion in the solution caused acidity? Tick (✓) **one** box. **[1 mark]**

- H^+ ☐
- SO_4^{2-} ☐
- Cu^{2+} ☐
- OH^- ☐

03.5 How did the pH of the solution change in the beaker? Tick (✓) **one** box. **[1 mark]**

- The pH started high and decreased to below 7. ☐
- The pH started low and increased to 7. ☐
- The pH stayed the same. ☐
- The pH started low and increased to above 7. ☐

0 4 This question is about carbon.

0 4 . 1 Graphite is commonly used as a lubricant in machines that operate at high temperatures.

Which properties of graphite explain why it is suitable for this use?
Tick (✓) **one** box. **[1 mark]**

Electrical conductor and high melting point ☐

Good heat and electrical conductor ☐

Good heat conductor and slippery ☐

High melting point and slippery ☐

0 4 . 2 Carbon nanotubes are cylindrical fullerenes.

Outline **two** important physical properties of nanotubes. **[2 marks]**

____

____

0 4 . 3 Diamond has a tetrahedral structure, as shown in **Figure 1**.

Figure 1

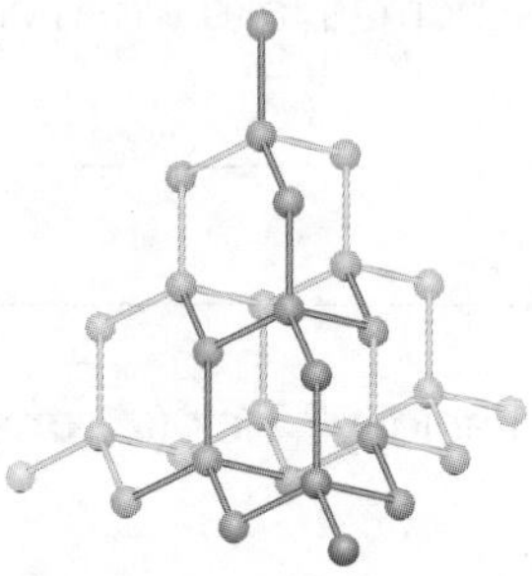

Explain why diamond has a very high melting point and why, unlike graphite, it does not conduct electricity. **[3 marks]**

____

____

____

0 5 This question is about atoms and ions.

0 5 . 1 Which of these statements about a neutral atom is always correct?
Tick (✓) **one** box. **[1 mark]**

It has the same number of electrons and neutrons. ☐

It has the same number of protons and neutrons. ☐

It has the same number of protons, neutrons and electrons. ☐

It has the same number of electrons and protons. ☐

0 5 . 2 Fe^{2+} ions are formed during some chemical reactions. Look at the information given below and then complete **Table 1**. **[1 mark]**

$$^{56}_{26}\mathbf{Fe}$$

Table 1

Number of protons in the ion	
Number of neutrons in the ion	
Number of electrons in the ion	

0 5 . 3 Explain how you worked out each of the three numbers. **[3 marks]**

Number of protons:

____

____

Number of neutrons:

____

____

Number of electrons:

____

____

0 5 . 4 **Figure 2** shows the electronic structure of an oxygen atom and a magnesium atom.

Figure 2

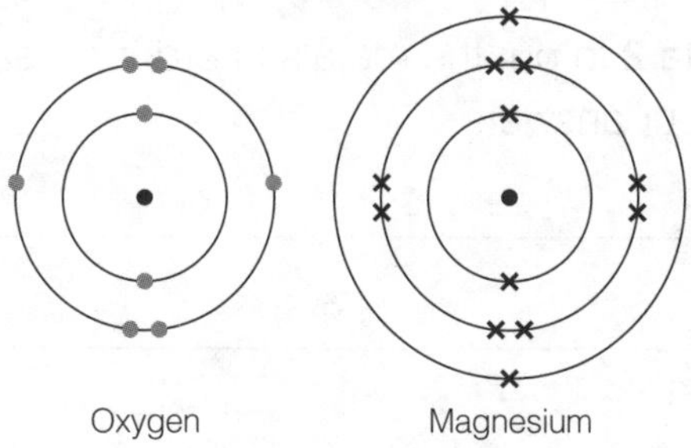

Electrons are transferred when magnesium burns in oxygen to produce magnesium oxide.

Describe how the magnesium atoms form magnesium ions and the oxygen atoms form oxide ions. **[2 marks]**

____

____

0 5 . 5 Give the charge of each ion. **[2 marks]**

____

____

0 6 Using a test tube, Ayesha and Jacob mixed citric acid with a solution of sodium hydrogen carbonate. They observed fizzing and the test tube got cooler.

0 6 . 1 Name the gas that was produced. **[1 mark]**

____

0 6 . 2 What type of reaction produces a decrease in temperature? **[1 mark]**

____

Ayesha and Jacob then investigated the temperature changes that occur when metals are added in excess to a solution of iron nitrate.

0 6 . 3 Why did Ayesha and Jacob need to add excess metal? **[1 mark]**

____

0 6 . 4 **Table 2** shows the results of their investigation.

Table 2

Metal	Temperature rise (°C)
Calcium	7.5
Copper	0.0
Zinc	3.2
Magnesium	5.8

Use the results from **Table 2** to put the metals in order of reactivity, starting with the most reactive metal. Explain your answer. **[3 marks]**

____

____

____

0 6 . 5 **Figure 3** shows the reaction profile of an exothermic reaction.

Figure 3

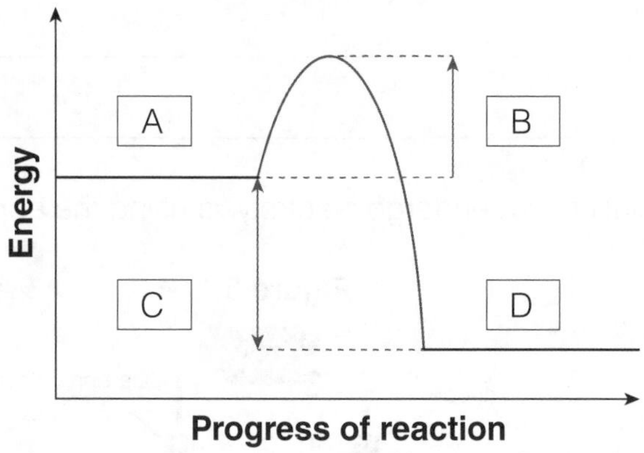

Write the correct letter next to the terms below, to show where they belong on **Figure 3**. **[3 marks]**

Activation energy ____________

Products ____________

Reactants ____________

Energy given out during the reaction ____________

0 7 . 1 The formula of copper carbonate is $CuCO_3$.

How many atoms are present in this formula? ______________________________ **[1 mark]**

0 7 . 2 Calculate the relative formula mass of copper carbonate. Show all your working.
The atomic mass of Cu is 64, C is 12 and O is 16. **[2 marks]**

____

____

0 7 . 3 Carbon dioxide is made by the thermal decomposition of copper(II) carbonate (see **Figure 4**).
Copper(II) oxide is also made.

Figure 4

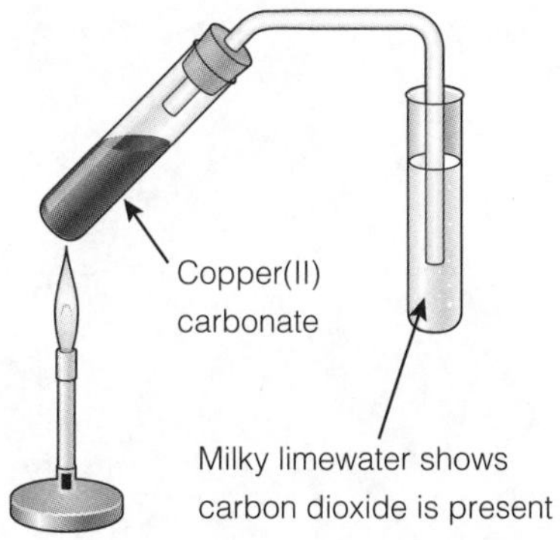

Write the word equation for the decomposition reaction. **[1 mark]**

____

0 7 . 4 Calculate the mass of carbon dioxide made when 12.35 g of copper(II) carbonate is heated to make 7.95 g of copper(II) oxide. Show your working. **[2 marks]**

____

____

0 8 Copper(II) sulfate solution can undergo electrolysis using the apparatus shown in **Figure 5**.

Figure 5

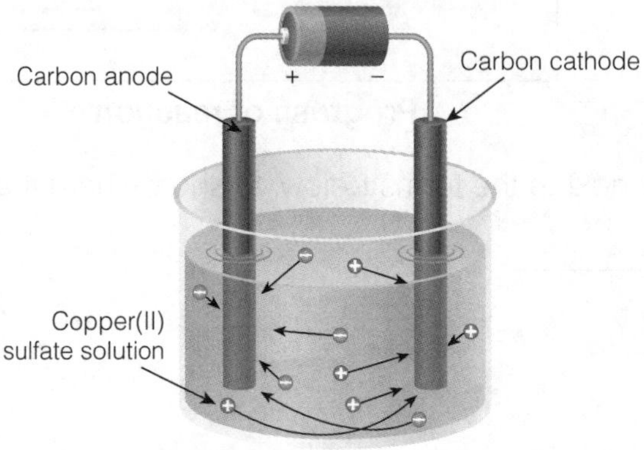

0 8 . 1 Describe the meaning of the term electrolysis. **[2 marks]**

____

____

0 8 . 2 Explain why copper sulfate crystals cannot be used during electrolysis. **[1 mark]**

____

0 8 . 3 During the reaction, a pink-coloured solid covered the cathode and bubbles were seen at the anode. Name the products seen at the anode and cathode. **[2 marks]**

____

____

0 8 . 4 Compare the electrolysis of molten sodium chloride with that of sodium chloride solution. Explain your answer. **[6 marks]**

0 9 This question is about group 7 elements.

0 9 . 1 Finlay added an aqueous solution of sodium iodide to a solution of bromine. The colour changed from orange to deep brown. Finlay then added an aqueous solution of sodium chloride to the bromine solution. The orange colour did not change. Explain these observations. **[4 marks]**

0 9 . 2 Chlorine is composed of diatomic molecules, Cl_2.
Draw a dot-and-cross diagram to show the bonding in a chlorine molecule. You should only show the outer shell electrons in your diagram. **[2 marks]**

0 9 . 3 Chlorine and iodine are both in group 7 of the periodic table.
Explain why chlorine is a gas and iodine is a solid at room temperature. **[2 marks]**

0 9 . 4 Explain why solid iodine does not conduct electricity. **[1 mark]**

END OF QUESTIONS

Letts

F

GCSE

COMBINED SCIENCE: TRILOGY

Foundation Tier Paper 4: Chemistry 2F

Time allowed: 1 hour 15 minutes

You may use:

- a ruler
- a calculator

Instructions

- Answer **all** questions in the spaces provided.
- Do all rough work in this book. Cross through any work you do not want to be marked.

Information

- There are 70 marks available on this paper.
- The marks for questions are shown in brackets.
- You are expected to use a calculator where appropriate.
- You are reminded of the need for good English and clear presentation in your answers.
- When answering question 06.1 you need to make sure that your answer:
  - is clear, logical, sensibly structured
  - fully meets the requirements of the question
  - shows that each separate point or step supports the overall answer.

Advice

- In all calculations, show clearly how you work out your answer.

Name: ....

0 1 This question is about some gases.

0 1 . 1 Which one of the following gases will bleach damp litmus paper? Tick (✓) **one** box. **[1 mark]**

Carbon dioxide ☐

Chlorine ☐

Hydrogen ☐

Methane ☐

0 1 . 2 Which one of the following gases is made when ethanoic acid reacts with calcium carbonate? Tick (✓) **one** box. **[1 mark]**

Carbon dioxide ☐

Chlorine ☐

Hydrogen ☐

Methane ☐

0 1 . 3 Carbon monoxide is a colourless, odourless gas. Which two pictograms would you associate with it? Tick (✓) **two** boxes. **[2 marks]**

A ☐

B ☐

C ☐

D ☐

E ☐

F ☐

0 1 . 4 What are the consequences of a person breathing in carbon monoxide? **[2 marks]**

____

____

0 1 . 5 Oxides of nitrogen cause acid rain. What other pollutant can cause acid rain? **[1 mark]**

____

0 1 . 6 What effects do acid rain have on the environment? **[2 marks]**

____

____

0 2 This question is about looking after the environment.

0 2 . 1 Which of these resources is not finite? Tick (✓) one box. **[1 mark]**

Natural gas ☐

Wood ☐

Iron ore ☐

Coal ☐

0 2 . 2 In the production of a pair of denim jeans, what is likely to have the biggest environmental impact?
Tick (✓) **one** box. **[1 mark]**

Extracting and processing the raw materials ☐

Manufacturing the jeans and packaging / labels / tags ☐

Wearing the jeans during its lifetime ☐

Disposing of the jeans at the end of its useful life ☐

0 2 . 3 Define what is meant by sustainable development. **[1 mark]**

____

____

0 2 . 4 In many parts of the world timber is used for houses. Evaluate whether timber is sustainable. **[2 marks]**

____

____

0 3 This question is about hydrocarbons.

0 3 . 1 Which of the following molecules has the formula C_4H_{10}? Tick (✓) **one** box. **[1 mark]**

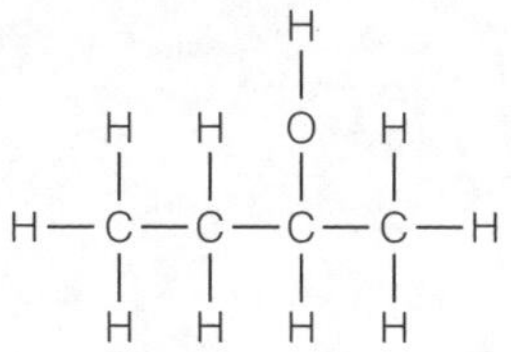 ☐

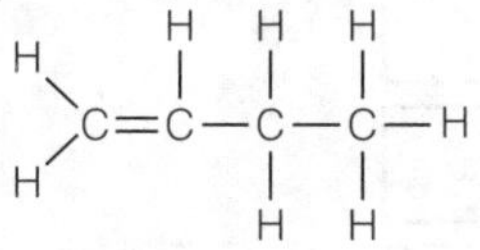 ☐

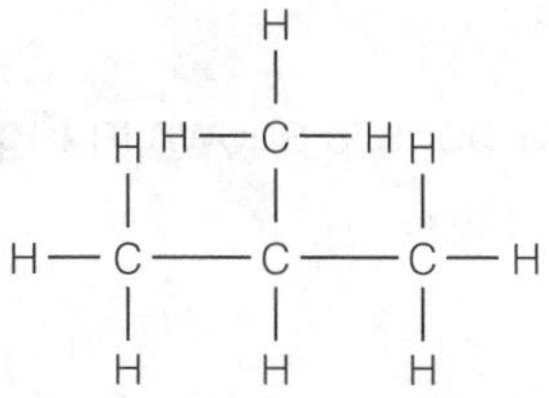 ☐

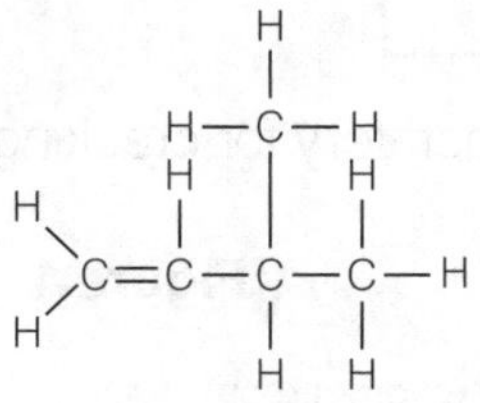 ☐

0 3 . 2 Crude oil is a mixture of hydrocarbons. It is separated into its components by fractional distillation.

Name two useful fractions that come from crude oil. **[2 marks]**

____

____

0 3 . 3 What is a hydrocarbon? **[2 marks]**

____

0 3 . 4 What two physical changes take place during distillation? Tick (✓) **two** boxes. **[2 marks]**

Melting ☐

Freezing ☐

Evaporation ☐

Condensation ☐

Sublimation ☐

0 3 . 5 The combustion of hydrocarbon fuels releases energy. Methane (CH_4) gas is one of the fuels used to heat our homes and cook our food. This word equation shows what happens when methane gas burns.

Methane + oxygen → carbon dioxide + water

Write a balanced symbol equation for the reaction. **[2 marks]**

____

0 3 . 6 During the combustion reaction, what happens to the carbon and hydrogen?
Tick (✓) **one** box. **[1 mark]**

They decompose. ☐

They are oxidised. ☐

They are reduced. ☐

They are neutralised. ☐

0 4 The apparatus used in the laboratory for cracking long-chain hydrocarbons is shown in **Figure 1**.

Figure 1

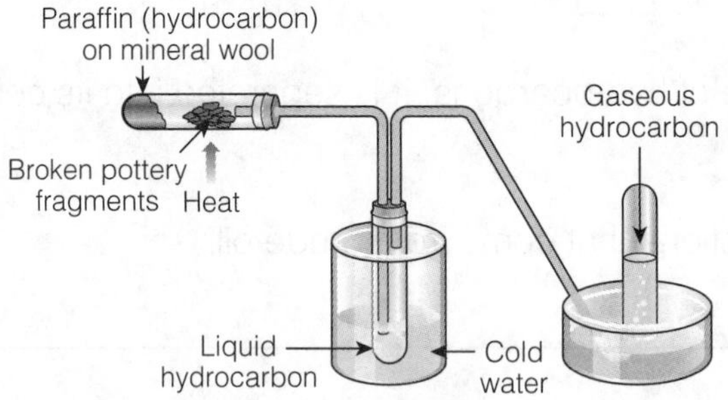

0 4 . 1 What is the purpose of the broken pottery fragments? **[1 mark]**

____

0 4 . 2 Explain what is meant by **cracking** long-chain hydrocarbons. **[2 marks]**

____

____

0 4 . 3 The paraffin on the mineral wool has the formula $C_{16}H_{34}$. The gaseous product is ethene (C_2H_4) and the liquid hydrocarbon is decane ($C_{10}H_{22}$).

Construct a balanced symbol equation for the reaction. **[2 marks]**

____

0 5 Five students each have a test tube containing 10 cm³ of hydrochloric acid of the same concentration. They each have a different-sized strip of magnesium ribbon.

They drop the magnesium into the acid and time how long it takes for the fizzing to stop.

Table 1 shows the results of the experiment.

Table 1

Student	Iram	Alex	Dylan	Georgie	Noah
Time (s)	246	258	204	300	272

0 5 . 1 Which student had the fastest reaction? **[1 mark]**

____

0 5 . 2 Georgie noticed that there was some magnesium left in the test tube when the fizzing stopped. In all the other test tubes, there was no magnesium left. Explain these two observations.

[2 marks]

____

____

____

0 5 . 3 Georgie repeated her experiment.

This time she measured the volume of gas made with a gas syringe. She measured 94.5 cm^3 of gas made in 225 seconds.

Calculate the mean rate of reaction. Show your working and include the unit in your answer.

[3 marks]

____

____

____

0 5 . 4 Georgie repeated her experiment again. This time she used double the volume of acid and double the amount of magnesium.

Predict what happened to the amount of gas made in the reaction. Explain your answer.

[2 marks]

____

____

____

0 6 **Figure 2** shows the result of a chromatography experiment on an unknown black ink.

In the experiment, Marie used:

- chromatography paper
- a hook to hang the paper on
- a chromatography tank and lid
- a pencil and ruler
- solvent
- five bottles of ink (A, B, C, D and unknown)
- a hairdryer.

Figure 2

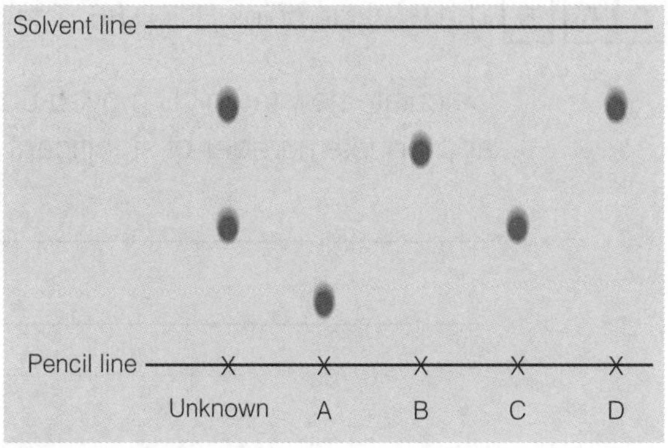

0 6 . 1 Write a method for the experiment that uses this equipment. **[6 marks]**

____

____

____

____

____

____

____

____

____

____

0 6 . 2 Which inks does the unknown ink in **Figure 2** contain?
Tick (✓) **one** box. **[1 mark]**

A and B ☐

A and C ☐

B and D ☐

C and D ☐

0 6 . 3 Which of the inks is the most soluble in the solvent? Give a reason for your answer. **[2 marks]**

____

____

0 6 . 4 What is meant by the term R_f value? **[1 mark]**

____

0 6 . 5 The R_f value of ink B is 0.86. The solvent line moved 7.91 cm from the pencil line.

Calculate how far ink B moved up the paper. Show your working. Give your answer to an appropriate number of significant figures. **[2 marks]**

____

____

0 7 This question is about the Earth's atmosphere.

0 7 . 1 Which pie chart shows the composition of the Earth's atmosphere today? Tick (✓) **one** box.

[1 mark]

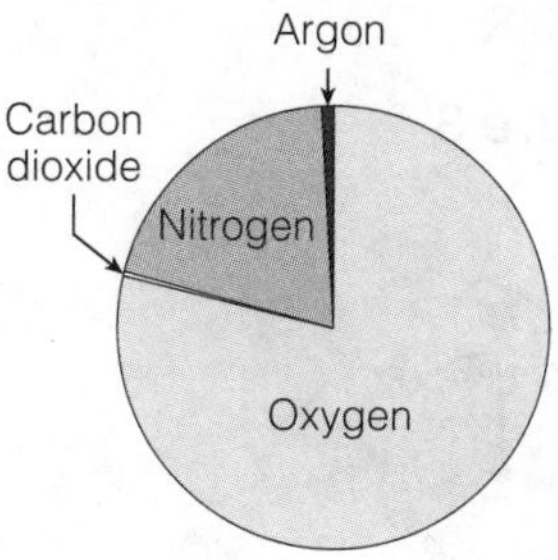

☐

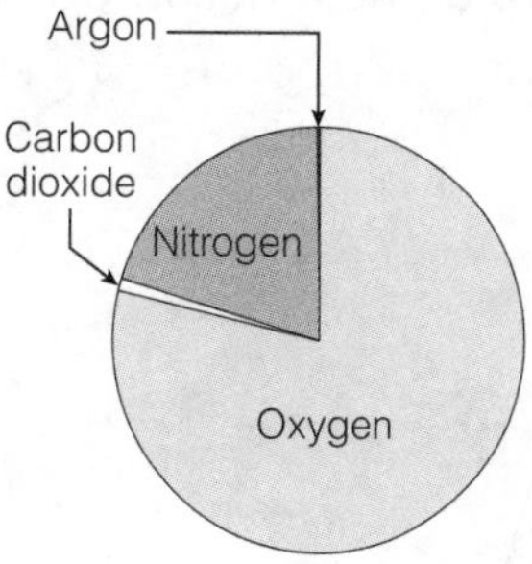

☐

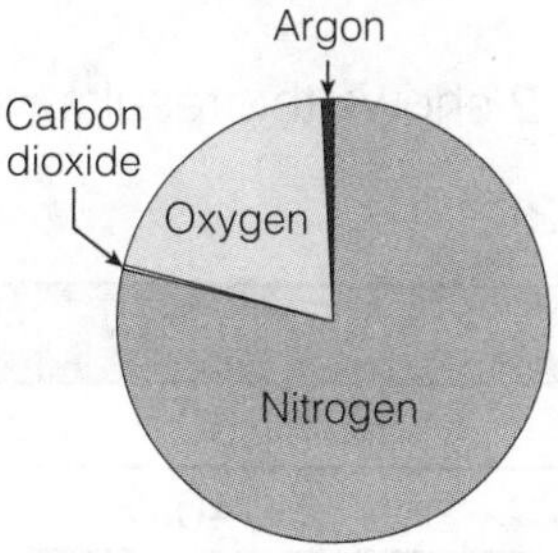

☐

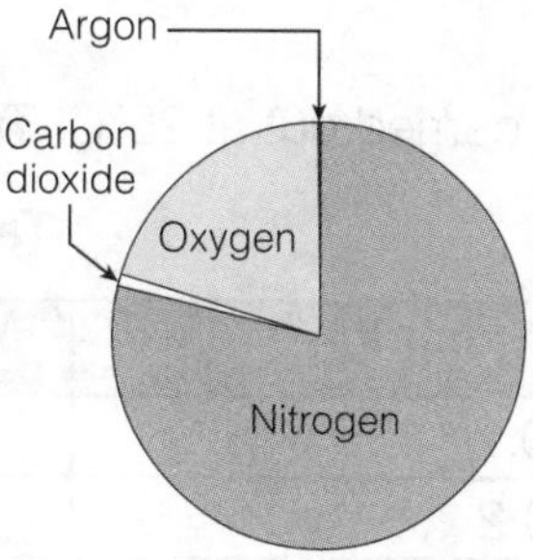

☐

0 7 . 2 These statements describe the process by which the Earth's atmosphere has changed since the Earth was formed.

A Oceans formed as the temperature at the surface fell below 100°C.

B Photosynthesis released oxygen into the atmosphere and used up carbon dioxide.

C Nitrifying bacteria used up ammonia and released nitrogen.

D Hot volcanic earth released carbon dioxide and ammonia into the atmosphere.

Put each letter in the correct box to show the order that scientists now believe the atmosphere developed.

[2 marks]

☐ → ☐ → ☐ → ☐

0 7 . 3 How the Earth's atmosphere evolved is a theory. What is a theory?

[2 marks]

____

____

0 7 . 4 Explain why the way that the Earth's atmosphere evolved can only be a theory.

[1 mark]

____

____

0 8 Meg carried out a rate of reaction experiment by reacting hydrochloric acid with sodium thiosulfate solution. A yellow precipitate of sulfur formed.

As shown in **Figure 3**, the reaction was followed by timing how long it took a cross drawn under a flask to disappear.

Figure 3

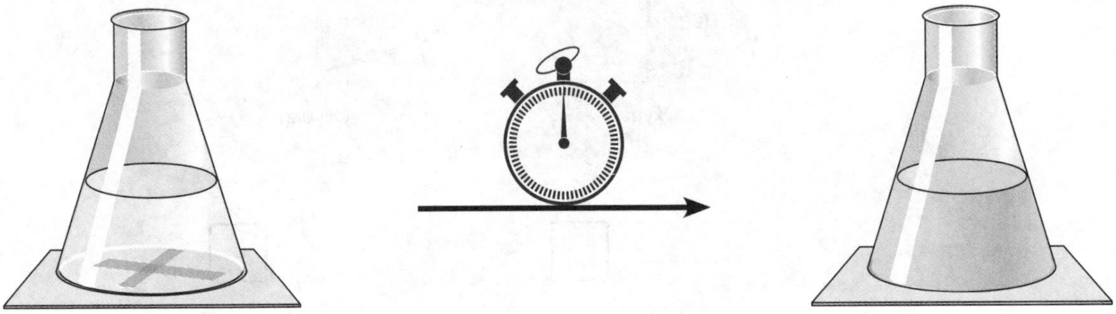

All reactions were carried out at 25°C. **Table 2** shows the results.

Table 2

Concentration of acid (mol/dm^3)	Time taken for cross to disappear (s)
0.1	60
0.2	40
0.4	24
0.6	13
0.8	8
1.0	4

0 8 . 1 Plot the results on the graph paper in **Figure 4**. **[3 marks]**

Figure 4

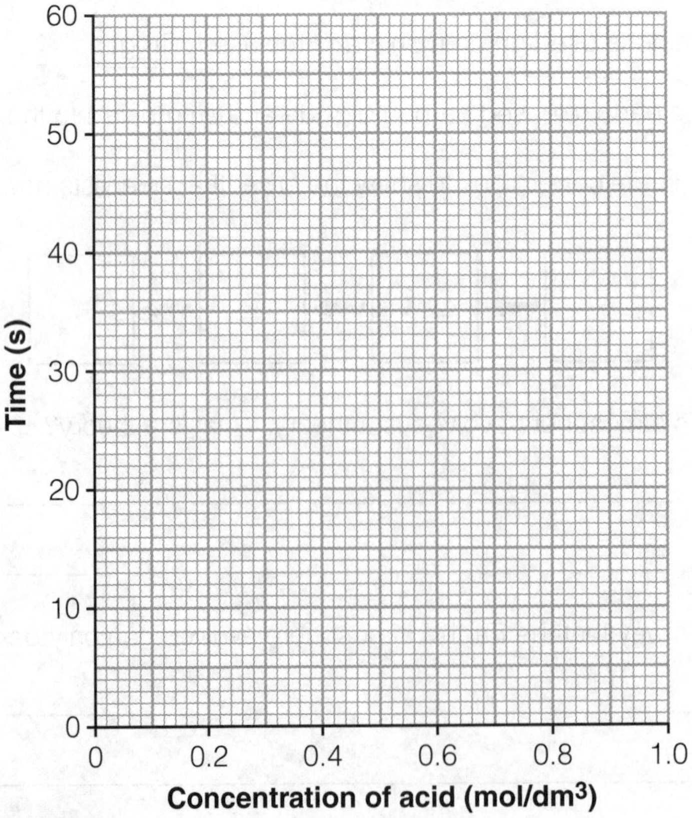

0 8 . 2 Describe and explain how the rate of reaction changes as the concentration of acid changes. **[3 marks]**

____

____

____

0 8 . 3 The experiment was repeated at 35°C. Predict how the reaction times would change. **[1 mark]**

____

0 9 Jessie heated some blue copper sulfate crystals. The crystals turned white and steam was given off.

0 9 . 1 What type of reaction took place? Tick (✓) **one** box. **[1 mark]**

Decomposition ☐

Endothermic ☐

Exothermic ☐

Oxidation ☐

0 9 . 2 The word equation for the reaction is:

hydrated copper sulfate (blue) $\rightleftharpoons$ anhydrous copper sulfate (white) + water

What does $\rightleftharpoons$ tell you about this reaction? **[1 mark]**

____

0 9 . 3 What should Jessie do to turn the white powder blue again? **[1 mark]**

____

1 0 **Figure 5** shows the results of an investigation into the reaction of zinc metal with hydrochloric acid.

Experiments A and B used 2 g of zinc: one experiment used zinc powder and the other used zinc granules.

Figure 5

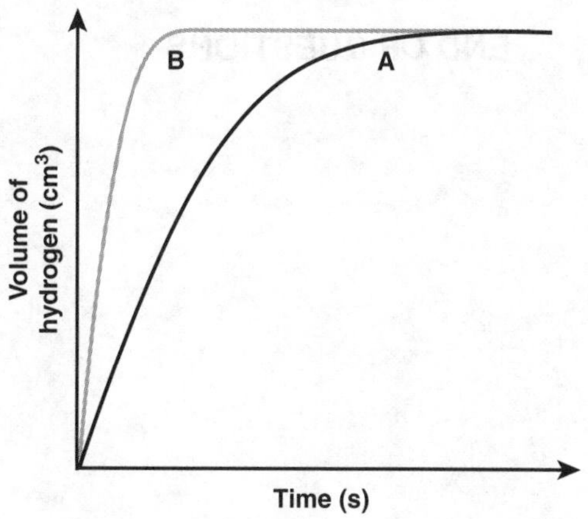

1 0 . 1 Which line on the graph represents the reaction with powdered zinc?
Explain your answer using the idea of reacting particles. **[4 marks]**

____

____

____

____

____

1 0 . 2 Copper ions (Cu^{2+}) act as a catalyst for the reaction.

Figure 6 shows the reaction profile without a catalyst.

Figure 6

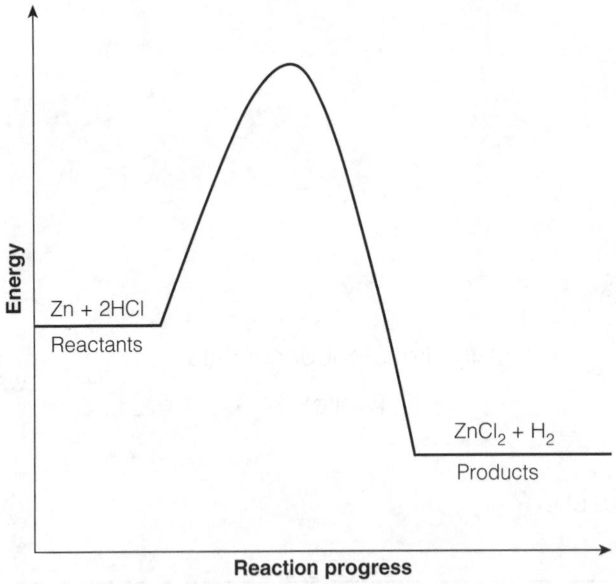

Draw on the graph the reaction profile with the catalyst. **[1 mark]**

____

END OF QUESTIONS

Letts

F

GCSE

COMBINED SCIENCE: TRILOGY

Foundation Tier   Paper 5: Physics 1F

Time allowed: 1 hour 15 minutes

You may use:

- a ruler
- a calculator
- the Physics Equation Sheet.

Instructions

- Answer **all** questions in the spaces provided.
- Do all rough work in this book. Cross through any work you do not want to be marked.

Information

- There are 70 marks available on this paper.
- The marks for questions are shown in brackets.
- You are expected to use a calculator where appropriate.
- You are reminded of the need for good English and clear presentation in your answers.
- When answering question 06.1 you need to make sure that your answer:
  - is clear, logical, sensibly structured
  - fully meets the requirements of the question
  - shows that each separate point or step supports the overall answer.

Advice

- In all calculations, show clearly how you work out your answer.

Name: ______________________________

0 1 This question is about circuits.

0 1 . 1 Look at the circuit diagram in **Figure 1**. Bulbs X and Y are identical.

Figure 1

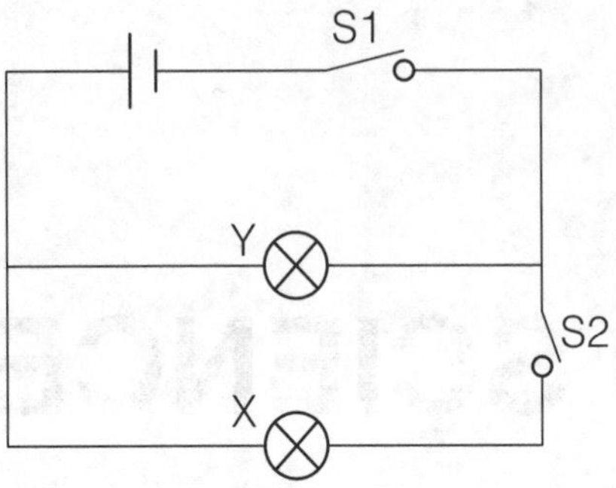

What happens to the bulbs when:

S1 is closed and S2 is open? ______________________ **[1 mark]**

S2 is closed and S1 is open? ______________________ **[1 mark]**

S1 and S2 are closed? ______________________ **[1 mark]**

0 1 . 2 Which of the following circuit diagram symbols represents a thermistor?
Tick (✓) **one** box. **[1 mark]**

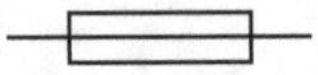 ☐

 ☐

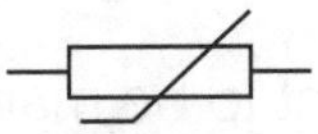 ☐

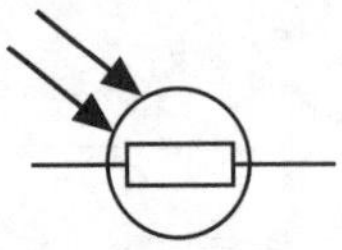 ☐

0 1 . 3 The diagrams show four circuits. Each circuit has two **identical** bulbs connected in parallel.

In which circuit will the ammeters have the same reading?
Tick (✓) **one** box. **[1 mark]**

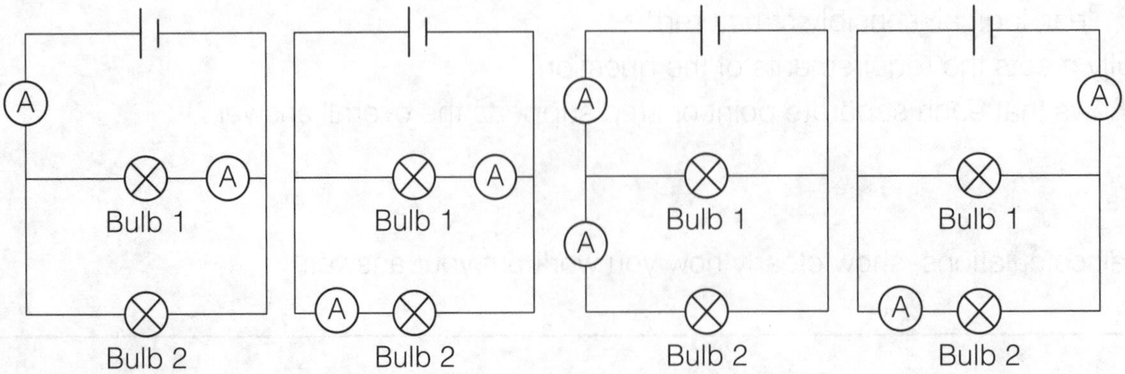

☐ ☐ ☐ ☐

0 1 . 4 A torch bulb has a resistance of 1200 Ω. The bulb operates when the current through it is 0.005 A. How many 1.5 V batteries will the torch need to operate? **[3 marks]**

____

____

____

0 1 . 5 Alex and Louise want to find out the identity of the mystery electrical component contained in Box Z. They connect it in the circuit shown in **Figure 2**.

Figure 2

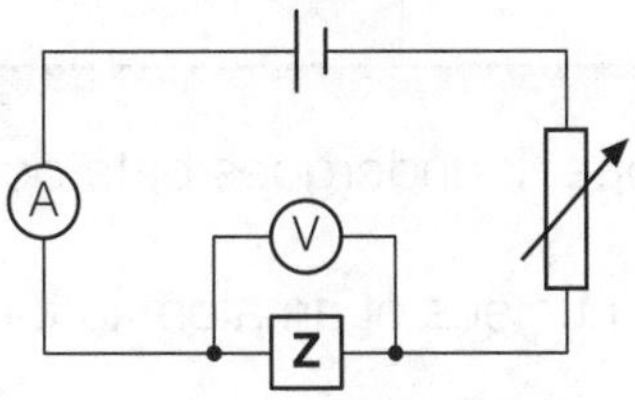

They change the potential difference, measure the current and plot the results (see **Figure 3**).

Figure 3

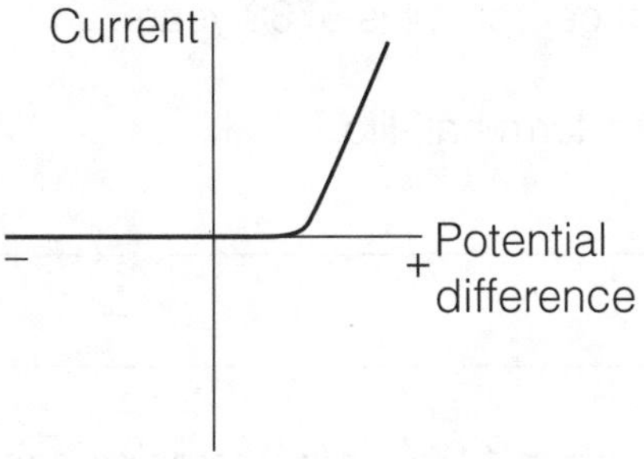

Write down the name of the mystery component in Box Z.
Explain your answer using ideas about resistance. **[3 marks]**

____

____

____

0 2 This question is about isotopes of carbon.

0 2 . 1 Complete **Table 1** to show the atomic structures of the three isotopes of carbon. **[3 marks]**

Table 1

Isotope	Number of protons	Number of neutrons	Number of electrons
Carbon-12	6	6	6
Carbon-13			
Carbon-14			

0 2 . 2 Carbon-14 is an unstable isotope. It undergoes beta decay to form nitrogen-14.

Describe what happens in the nucleus of an atom to form a beta particle. **[2 marks]**

____

____

0 2 . 3 The half-life for the decay of carbon-14 is 5730 years.

Explain what is meant by the term half-life. **[1 mark]**

____

____

0 2 . 4 The very small amount of carbon-14 in a plant remains constant until the plant dies. The amount of carbon-14 then falls steadily as the plant decays. The amount of carbon-12 stays the same.

The plant material can be dated by measuring the ratio of carbon-14 to carbon-12.

Complete **Table 2**. **[1 mark]**

Table 2

Number of half-lives	Time after death of organism in years	$^{14}C : {}^{12}C$ ratio / 10^{-12}
0	0	1.000
1	5730	0.500
2	11 460	0.250
3	____________	0.125

0 2 . 5 Use the data from **Table 2** to plot a decay curve for carbon-14 (see **Figure 4**). **[2 marks]**

Figure 4

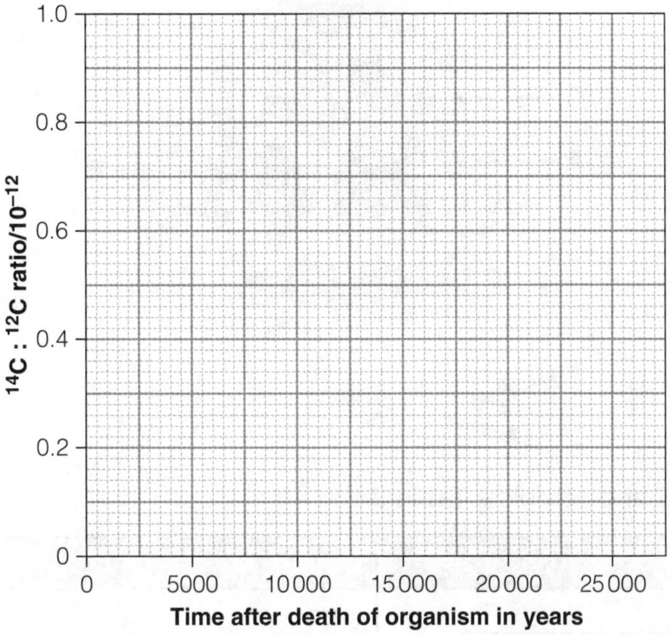

0 2 . 6 A sample of wood taken from an old shipwreck had a carbon-14 : carbon-12 ratio/10^{-12} of 0.3.

Use **Figure 4** to estimate the age of the wood. **[1 mark]**

____

0 3 This question is about electrical appliances.

0 3 . 1 Look at **Figure 5**. Which set of conditions would you find on the label of a microwave oven that operates with the mains electricity supply in the UK?
Tick (✓) **one** box. **[1 mark]**

50 Hz, 230 V, ac ☐

50 Hz, 230 V, dc ☐

60 Hz, 230 V, dc ☐

60 Hz, 230 V, ac ☐

Figure 5

0 3 . 2 **Figure 6** shows a symbol found on hairdryers.

Figure 6

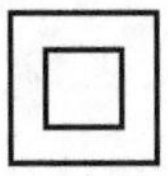

The symbol shows that the hairdryer is double insulated. What does this mean? Tick (✓) **one** box.
[1 mark]

It has a moulded plastic plug. ☐

It does not need an earth wire. ☐

The case has metal parts on the outside. ☐

The dryer has double plastic coating on the wires. ☐

Look at the diagram of a three-pin plug in **Figure 7**.

Figure 7

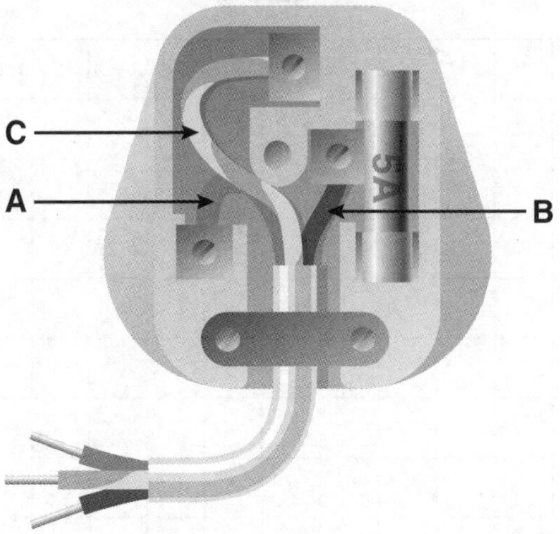

0 3 . 3 Look at **Figure 7** and complete **Table 3**. **[2 marks]**

Wire	Name	Colour
A	____________	Blue
B	Live	____________
C	____________	Green and yellow stripes

0 3 . 4 Give **three** reasons why wire C is connected to some domestic appliances. **[3 marks]**

____

____

____

0 4 This question is about energy resources.

0 4 . 1 Which of the following energy resources is non-renewable? Tick (✓) **one** box. **[1 mark]**

Bio-fuel ☐

Coal ☐

Hydro-electricity ☐

Wind ☐

0 4 . 2 Which of the following energy resources can be most relied on to give a constant supply of energy? Tick (✓) **one** box. **[1 mark]**

Geothermal ☐

Tidal ☐

Wave ☐

Wind ☐

0 4 . 3 State **one** environmental issue associated with the use of non-renewable fuels. **[1 mark]**

___

0 4 . 4 Give **two** reasons why we still use non-renewable fuels. **[2 marks]**

___

___

0 5 Look at the picture of the roller coaster in **Figure 8**.

Figure 8

0 5 . 1 At what position have the roller coaster cars got maximum kinetic energy?
Tick (✓) **one** box. **[1 mark]**

Position 1 ☐

Position 2 ☐

Position 3 ☐

Position 4 ☐

0 5 . 2 At position 1, the roller coaster is 100 m high, the cars have a mass of 520 kg and the gravitational field strength is 10 N/kg. Calculate the gravitational potential energy. Start by writing down the correct equation. **[3 marks]**

___

___

___

0 5 . 3 Describe the energy changes that take place as the roller coaster cars travel from position 1 to position 4. **[2 marks]**

___

___

0 6 Sally was asked to heat a sample of olive oil and a sample of vegetable oil and compare how the temperature changed.

This is the apparatus she used to carry out the experiment:

- 250 ml beaker
- thermometer
- tripod
- gauze
- bunsen burner
- clamp and stand
- stopwatch
- two boiling tubes with oil already in the bottom: 1 labelled 20 g olive oil and the other 20 g vegetable oil.

0 6 . 1 Describe how Sally should use this apparatus to carry out the experiment. **[6 marks]**

0 6 . 2 What safety precautions should Sally take? **[2 marks]**

0 6 . 3 Use the data in **Table 4** to predict which oil would show the greatest rise in temperature during the experiment. Give a reason for your answer. **[3 marks]**

Table 4

Type of oil	Olive oil	Vegetable oil
Specific heat capacity J/kg °C	1670	1970

0 7 This question is about the three states of matter.

0 7 . 1 How are the particles arranged in ice, water and water vapour? **[3 marks]**

Ice: ______________________________

Water: ______________________________

Water vapour: ______________________________

0 7 . 2 When a block of ice is left in the sunshine, it melts.

Explain what happens to the particles of ice during melting. **[4 marks]**

____

____

____

____

0 7 . 3 What is the term for the amount of energy needed to change from solid to liquid?
Tick (✓) **one** box. **[1 mark]**

Specific latent heat ☐

Specific latent heat of fusion ☐

Specific latent heat of vaporisation ☐

Specific heat capacity ☐

0 8 **Figure 9** shows some meteorites that Mahri is investigating.

Figure 9

0 8 . 1 Draw a labelled diagram to describe how she can measure the volume of each meteorite. **[2 marks]**

0 8 . 2 Mahri measures the volume of each meteorite three times. How does this improve her results?

[2 marks]

____

____

0 8 . 3 What other measurement does Mahri need to take so that she can calculate the density of the meteorites?

[1 mark]

____

0 8 . 4 **Table 5** shows the densities of common elements found in meteorites.

Table 5

Element	Density kg/m³
Aluminium	2712
Iron	7850
Magnesium	1738
Nickel	8908
Silicon	2328

The mean density of the three meteorites was 7965 kg/m³. Analysis indicated that two elements were present. Iron formed 90% of the composition. What was the element making up the remaining 10%?

Tick (✓) **one** box.

[1 mark]

Aluminium ☐

Magnesium ☐

Nickel ☐

Silicon ☐

0 9 Look at **Table 6**, which shows the specific heat capacity of four metals.

Table 6

Metal	Aluminium	Copper	Iron	Lead
Specific heat capacity J/kg °C	900	490	390	130

0 9 . 1 If you were given a 2 kg block of each metal, which metal would take the least amount of energy to raise its temperature from 20°C to 25°C?
Tick (✓) **one** box. **[1 mark]**

Aluminium ☐

Copper ☐

Iron ☐

Lead ☐

0 9 . 2 As shown in **Figure 10**, a 500 g block of copper was heated with a 100 W electric immersion heater for 85 seconds.

Figure 10

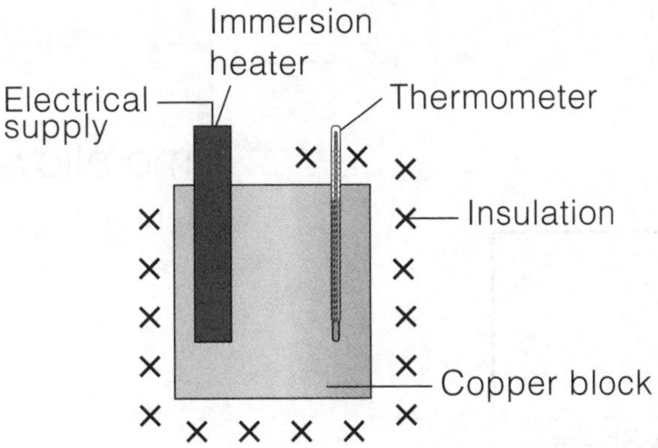

Calculate the amount of energy in joules supplied to the copper block. Show all your working.
[2 marks]

____

____

____

0 9 . 3 In a repeat experiment, the copper block started at a temperature of 22°C and was supplied with 9065 J of energy. What was its final temperature? Show all your working. **[3 marks]**

change in thermal energy = mass × specific heat capacity × temperature change

____

____

____

END OF QUESTIONS

Letts

F

GCSE

COMBINED SCIENCE: TRILOGY

Foundation Tier Paper 6: Physics 2F

Time allowed: 1 hour 15 minutes

You may use:

- a ruler
- a calculator
- the Physics Equation Sheet.

Instructions

- Answer **all** questions in the spaces provided.
- Do all rough work in this book. Cross through any work you do not want to be marked.

Information

- There are 70 marks available on this paper.
- The marks for questions are shown in brackets.
- You are expected to use a calculator where appropriate.
- You are reminded of the need for good English and clear presentation in your answers.
- When answering question 08.1 you need to make sure that your answer:
  - is clear, logical, sensibly structured
  - fully meets the requirements of the question
  - shows that each separate point or step supports the overall answer.

Advice

- In all calculations, show clearly how you work out your answer.

Name: ______________________________

0 1 Navjot and Shaleen are investigating the forces in floating and sinking.

Figure 1

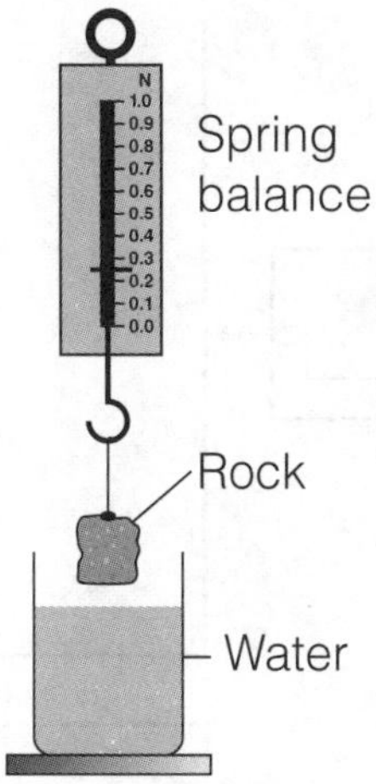

0 1 . 1 What is the weight of the rock shown in **Figure 1**? **[1 mark]**

0 1 . 2 What is the resolution of the newton meter?
Tick (✓) **one** box. **[1 mark]**

0.1 N ☐

0.5 N ☐

1.0 N ☐

5.0 N ☐

0 1 . 3 In this investigation there are several variables.
Draw one line from each variable to the correct description for this investigation. **[2 marks]**

Dependent variable	rock
Independent variable	distance lowered
Control variable	force /N

0 1 . 4 Describe what happens to the reading on the spring balance as Navjot and Shaleen slowly lower the rock into the water until it is fully submerged. **[2 marks]**

____

____

0 1 . 5 Navjot and Shaleen want to produce a graph to show how the force changes. Describe how they can improve their method to produce data that can be plotted on a line graph. **[2 marks]**

____

____

0 1 . 6 Label the axes on **Figure 2** to show how Navjot and Shaleen could plot their results. **[1 mark]**

Figure 2

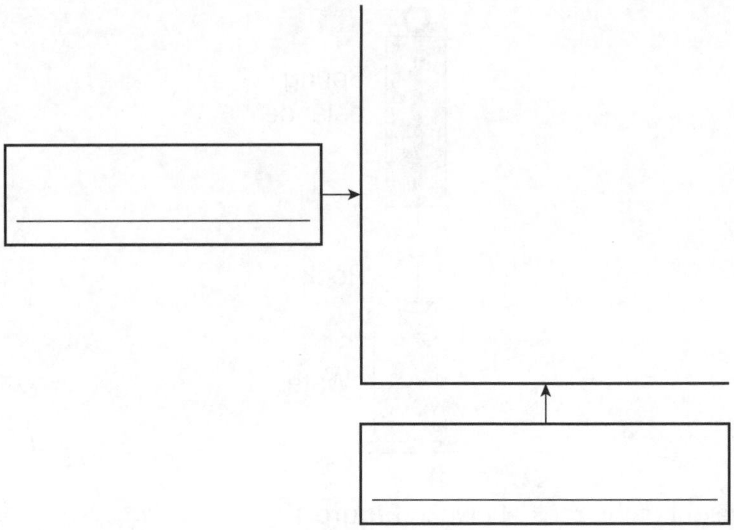

0 2 . 1 **Figure 3** shows an astronaut doing a spacewalk. He can move about using small jets of air blown in directions A, B, C and D. He is stationary.

Figure 3

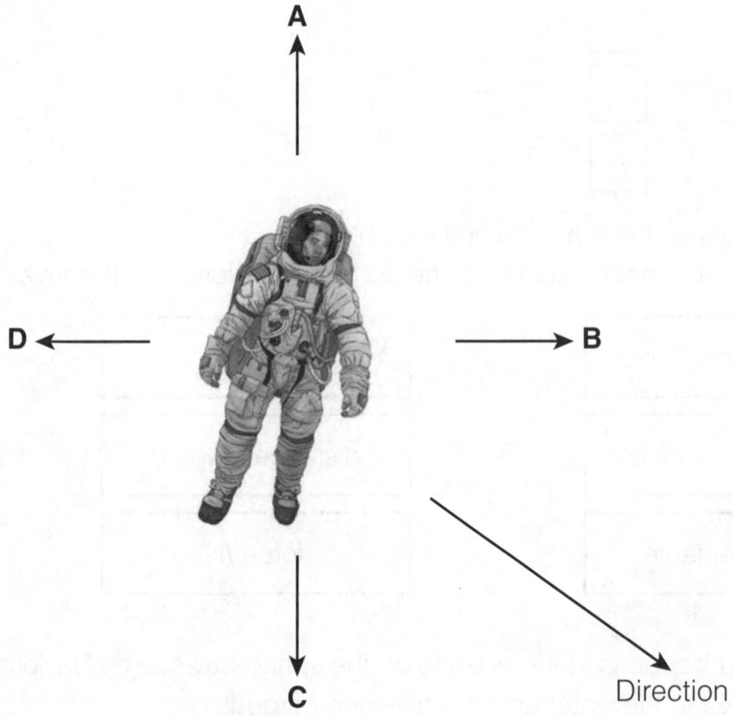

Which two jets should the astronaut use to move in the direction of the arrow shown?
Tick (✓) **one** box. **[1 mark]**

A and B ☐

A and D ☐

B and C ☐

C and D ☐

Figure 4 shows a skydiver.

Figure 4

0 2 . 2 X and Y are forces acting on the skydiver as she falls. Describe what happens to the size of force X as she accelerates. **[1 mark]**

____

0 2 . 3 The skydiver has a mass of 55 kg and the gravitational field strength is 10 N/kg. What is her weight? **[1 mark]**

____

0 2 . 4 What will be the value of force X when she stops accelerating and falls at terminal velocity? Explain your answer. **[2 marks]**

____

____

0 2 . 5 **Figure 5** shows the velocity of the skydiver as she descends through the air.

Figure 5

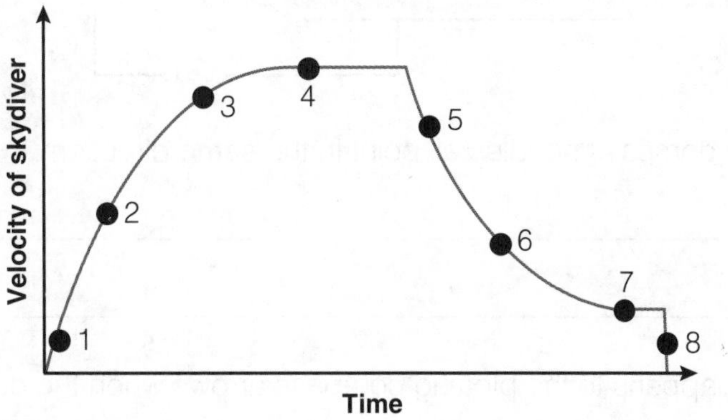

Between which two points does the skydiver open her parachute?
Tick (✓) **one** box. **[1 mark]**

4 and 5 ☐

5 and 6 ☐

6 and 7 ☐

7 and 8 ☐

0 3 . 1 **Figure 6** illustrates an experiment to show a magnetic field around a bar magnet using plotting compasses.

Figure 6

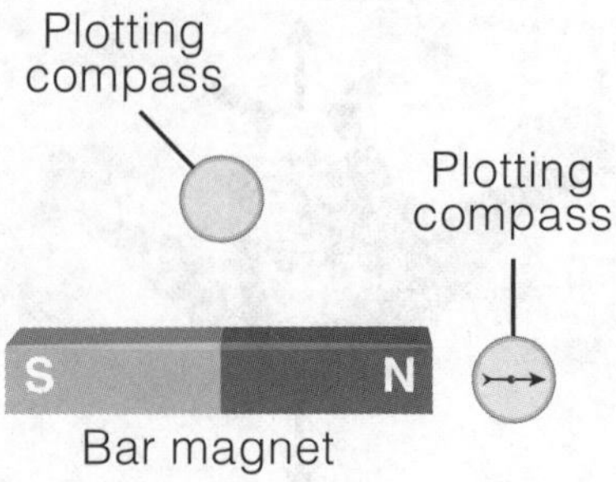

Which direction will the arrow point in the top plotting compass?

Tick (✓) **one** box. **[1 mark]**

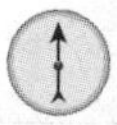	☐	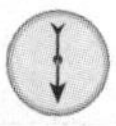	☐
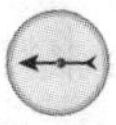	☐	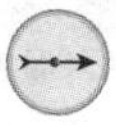	☐

Look at **Figure 7**.

Figure 7

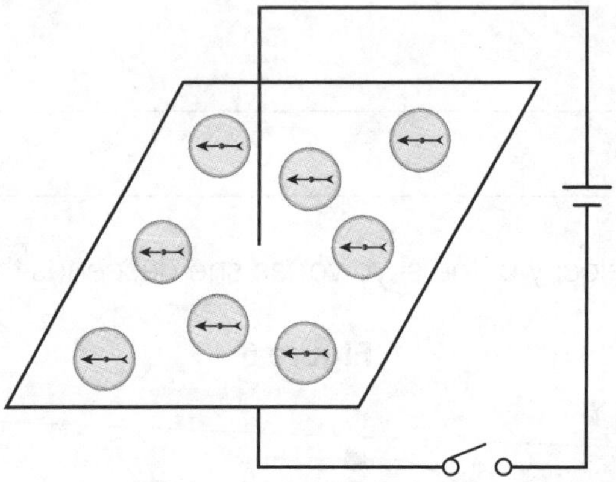

0 3 . 2 Explain why the compass needles all point in the same direction. **[2 marks]**

____

____

0 3 . 3 Describe what happens to the plotting compass arrows when the current is switched on. **[2 marks]**

____

____

Raj is trying to make an electromagnet that will pick up as many paper clips as possible.

First, he experiments with different materials to find out which ones are magnetic.

0 3 . 4 Which of these materials are magnetic? Tick (✓) **two** boxes. **[2 marks]**

Iron ☐

Plastic ☐

Zinc ☐

Ceramic ☐

Steel ☐

Copper ☐

0 3 . 5 Raj then sets up the circuit in **Figure 8** and switches on the power supply. He wants to know what the magnetic field looks like, so he uses a plotting compass to draw out the lines.

Figure 8

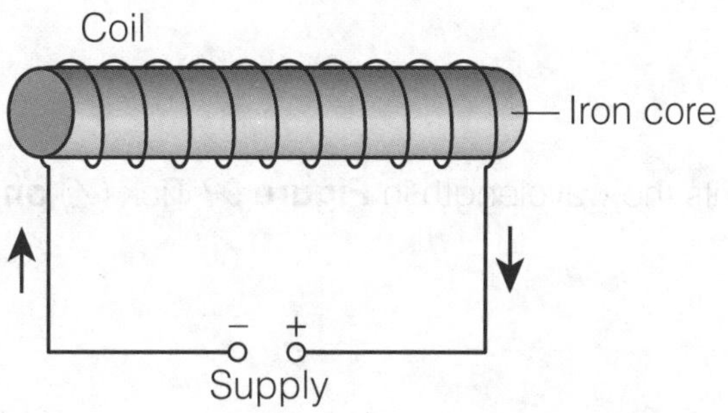

Draw the magnetic field lines on the diagram. **[3 marks]**

0 3 . 6 Raj wants to increase the strength of the electromagnet so that it can pick up more paper clips. What could he do? **[2 marks]**

____

____

0 3 . 7 Electromagnetics have many uses. Name **two**. **[2 marks]**

____

____

0 4 This question is about waves.

0 4 . 1 Look at **Figure 9**, which shows a wave.

Figure 9

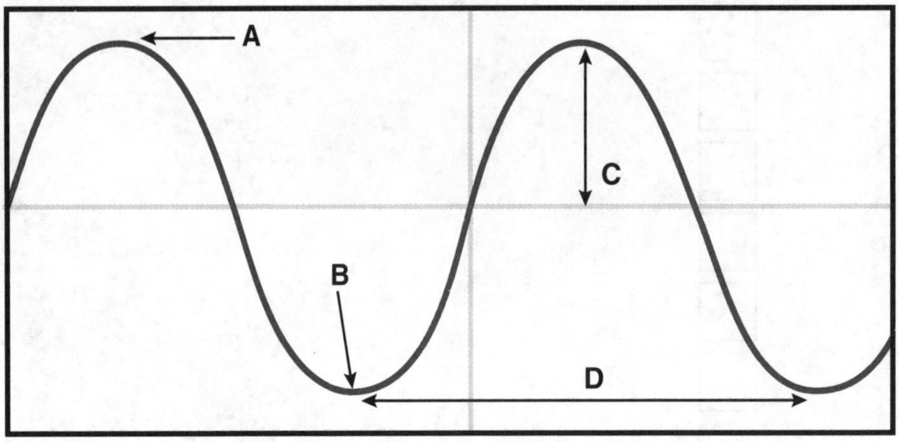

Which letter represents the amplitude of the wave?
Tick (✓) **one** box. **[1 mark]**

A ☐

B ☐

C ☐

D ☐

0 4 . 2 Which letter represents the wavelength in **Figure 9**? Tick (✓) **one** box. **[1 mark]**

A ☐

B ☐

C ☐

D ☐

0 4 . 3 Microwaves can be used to cook food in a microwave oven, shown in **Figure 10**.
Microwaves are part of the electromagnetic spectrum.

Figure 10

Which other part of the electromagnetic spectrum is commonly used to cook food? **[1 mark]**

____

0 4 . 4 The microwaves used in ovens have a wavelength of 0.12 m.

The speed of electromagnetic waves is 3×10^8 m/s.

What is the equation relating frequency, wave speed and wavelength? **[1 mark]**

____

____

0 4 . 5 Use the equation to calculate the frequency of the microwaves used in ovens. Show your working and include the unit in your answer. **[2 marks]**

____

____

____

0 5 Look at **Figure 11**, which shows a velocity–time graph of a car travelling on a road.

Figure 11

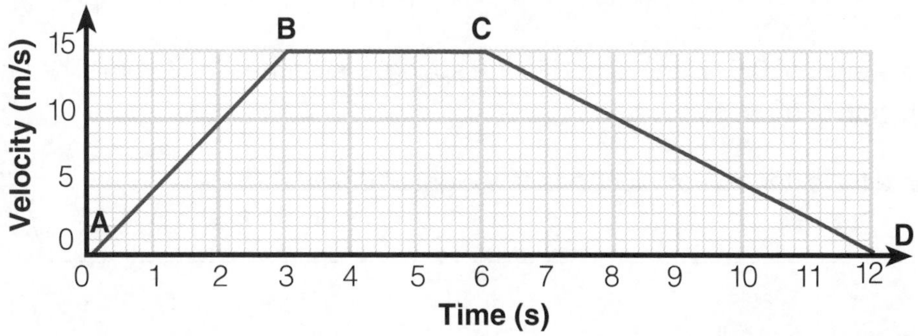

0 5 . 1 What is the velocity of the car after two seconds? **[1 mark]**

____

0 5 . 2 Calculate the acceleration of the car between points **A** and **B**.
Show all your working and include the unit in your answer. **[3 marks]**

____

____

____

____

0 5 . 3 Calculate the distance travelled between 0 and 6 seconds. Show all your working. **[3 marks]**

____

____

____

0 5 . 4 Describe the motion of the car between points **C** and **D**. **[2 marks]**

____

____

0 6 Hugh is investigating the stretching of a spring, using the apparatus shown in **Figure 12**.

Figure 12

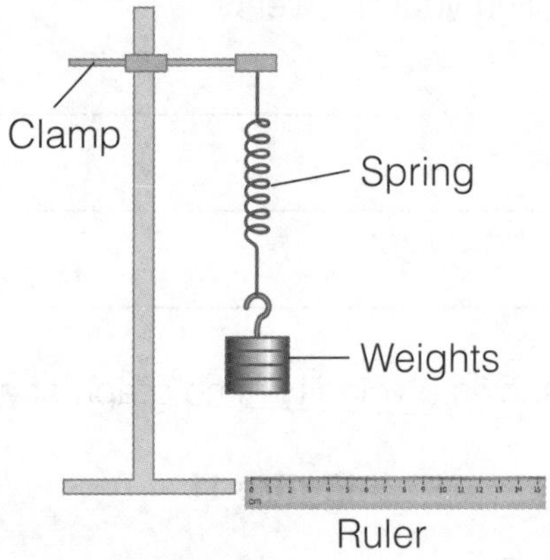

0 6 . 1 When a weight of 0.5 N is attached to the spring, it stretches to 62 mm. The unstretched spring has a length of 52 mm.

Calculate the extension produced by a weight of 0.5 N. **[1 mark]**

____

Hugh uses different weights in the investigation. **Table 1** shows the results.

Table 1

Weight (N)	Extension (mm)
0.2	4.0
0.4	8.0
0.6	12.0
0.8	16.0
1.0	20.0
1.2	24.0

0 6 . 2 Use the readings in **Table 1** to draw a graph of the results. **[3 marks]**

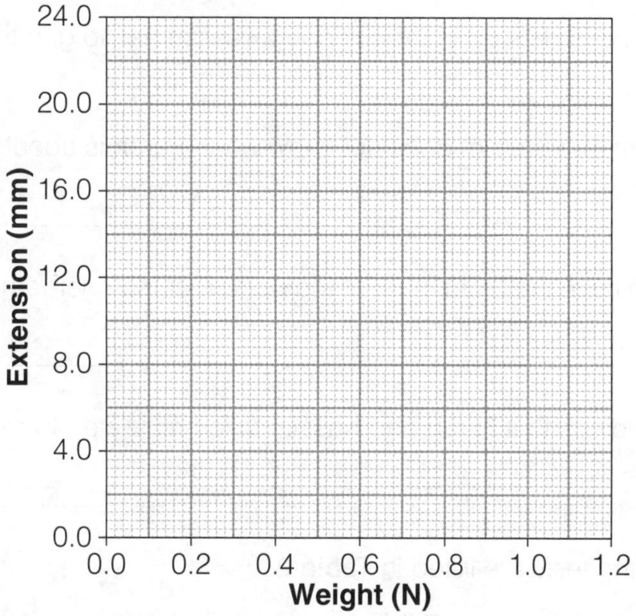

0 6 . 3 Use the graph to determine the force needed to cause an extension in the spring of 14 mm. **[1 mark]**

____

0 6 . 4 What conclusion can be drawn from the graph about stretching a spring? **[2 marks]**

____

____

0 6 . 5 Suggest how this investigation could be improved. **[2 marks]**

____

____

0 7 Farah and Kassim are testing their reaction times using a ruler.

Farah holds the ruler above her friend's hand, as shown in **Figure 13**.

Figure 13

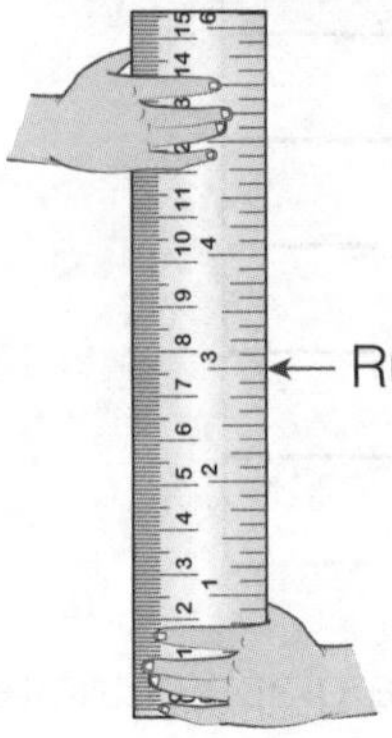

Without warning, Farah lets go of the ruler and Kassim has to grip the ruler as quickly as possible.

0 7 . 1 Why is it important that Kassim does not know when Farah is about to drop the ruler? **[1 mark]**

____

0 7 . 2 Why is it better to have the 0 cm mark at the bottom of the ruler rather than the top? **[1 mark]**

____

0 7 . 3 State how the readings that Farah and Kassim take are related to reaction time. **[1 mark]**

____

The results from the tests are listed in **Table 2**.

Table 2

	Distance dropped (cm)			
	Trial 1	**Trial 2**	**Trial 3**	**Average**
Kassim	11.0	20.0	12.0	11.5
Farah	15.0	16.0	14.0	

0 7 . 4 Calculate the average distance dropped for Farah. Show your working. **[2 marks]**

____

____

0 7 . 5 Identify the anomalous result and suggest a reason for it. **[2 marks]**

____

____

0 7 . 6 Give one conclusion that can be drawn from the results. **[1 mark]**

____

0 7 . 7 Kassim and Farah are keen swimmers and often take part in swimming galas.

When they race against each other, who do you think usually gets the best start to the race and why? **[3 marks]**

____

____

____

0 8 A car driver's awareness of stopping distances is an important part of driving safely.

0 8 . 1 The thinking distance and the braking distance can be affected by different factors. Explain how speed, alcohol and road conditions can affect driving safety. **[6 marks]**

____

____

____

____

____

____

____

____

____

____

____

END OF QUESTIONS

THIS IS A BLANK PAGE

THIS IS A BLANK PAGE

THIS IS A BLANK PAGE

Answers

Biology

CELL BIOLOGY

Page 6

1. **(a)** Nucleus **(1)**
   (b) Mitochondria are too small to see with a light microscope / require an electron microscope / resolution of microscope not high enough. **(1)**
   (c) Liver cells require the release of a lot of energy **(1)**; mitochondria release energy for muscle contraction **(1)**.
   (d) Cell, cytoplasm, nucleus, chromosome, gene **(2 marks for everything in the correct order, 1 mark if cell, cytoplasm and nucleus are in the correct order, reading left to right)**
2. **(a)** Bacteria have a chromosomal loop; have plasmids; no nuclear membrane / nucleus. **(1)**
   (b) Prokaryotic ✓ **(1)**

Page 7

1. **(a)** An undifferentiated cell that can develop into one of many different types. **(1)**
   (b) **Any two from:** nucleus, cytoplasm, cell / plasma membrane, mitochondria, ribosomes. **(2)**
2. **(a)** **Any two from:** therapeutic cloning, treating paralysis, repairing nerve damage, cancer research, grow new organs for transplantation. **(2)**
   (b) **Any one from:** stem cells are sometimes obtained from human embryos and people believe it is wrong to use embryos for this purpose, risk of viral infections. **(1)**
3. $\frac{3600}{30} \times 200$ **(1)** = 24 000 μm **(1)** = 24 mm **(1)**

Page 8

1. **(a)** Line should point to one of the objective lenses / rotating nose cone. **(1)**
   (b) The organelles are too small to see **(1)** / microscope doesn't have a high enough resolving power. **(1)**
   (c) Size of real object = $\frac{3}{400}$ **(1)** = 0.0075 cm **(1)** = 75 μm **(1)**
2. **(a)** Scanning electron microscope **(1)**
   (b) **For 2 marks, accept any answer between 80–100 minutes**; if answer is incorrect, award 1 mark for the idea that there have been 4 divisions.

Page 9

1. **Any two from:** specialised organs carry out a specific job; multicellular organisms are complex and require specialised organs so they can grow larger; single-celled organisms are small enough not to require specialised cells and transport systems. **(2)**
2.

Mitosis	Meiosis
Involved in asexual reproduction	**Involved in sexual reproduction (1)**
Produces clones / no variation (1)	Produces variation
Produces cells with 46 chromosomes	**Produces cells with 23 chromosomes (1)**

3. **(a)** Meiosis **(1)**
   (b) Four cells produced (in second meiotic division) **(1)**
4. **(a)** Benign tumours don't spread from the original site of cancer in the body **(1)**; Malignant tumour cells invade neighbouring tissues / spread to other parts of the body / form secondary tumours. **(1)**
   (b) **Any two from:** not smoking tobacco products; not drinking too much alcohol; avoiding exposure to UV rays; eating a healthy diet; taking moderate exercise / reduce obesity. **(2)**

Page 10

1. glucose + oxygen ⟶ carbon dioxide + water **(1 mark for correct reactants; 1 mark for products)**
2. **(a)** **Any two from:** larger athletes will use more oxygen due to their higher muscle mass; the adjustment allows rates to be fairly / accurately compared; different athletes may have different masses. **(2)**
   (b) Sprinting has a greater energy demand **(1)**, so more oxygen is needed **(1)**.
   (c) Boris' consumption rate would be lower **(1)** because his lungs, heart and muscles are less efficient at transporting / using oxygen **(1)**.

Page 11

1. **(a)**

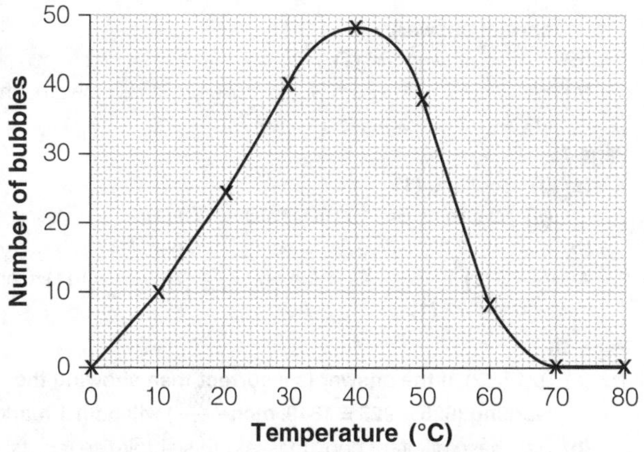

(2 marks for correct plotting; 1 mark for smooth curve; subtract 1 mark for every incorrect plot)

   (b) The rate of bubbles produced increases until it reaches an optimum / maximum **(1)**; then it decreases rapidly, producing no bubbles at 70°C **(1)**.
   (c) 40°C **(1)**
   (d) **Any two from:** enzyme / active site has changed shape / become denatured; substrate / hydrogen peroxide no longer fits active site, so substrate cannot be broken down; low pH of the stomach **or** amylase works best at alkaline pH and stomach is acid. **(2)**

TRANSPORT SYSTEMS AND PHOTOSYNTHESIS

Page 12

1. **(a)** **Any two named small nutrient molecules**, e.g. glucose, vitamins, minerals, ions, amino acids, oxygen **(2)**.
   (b) **Any one from:** carbon dioxide or urea. **(1)**
2. **(a)** Water moves down concentration gradient from high water concentration to low water concentration **(1)**, across a partially / differentially permeable membrane / plasma membrane **(1)**; gradient maintained by input and output of water at each end of cell line **(1)**.
   (b) Water moving from plant cell to plant cell ✓ **(1)**; A pear losing water in a concentrated solution of sugar ✓ **(1)**; Water moving from blood plasma to body cells ✓ **(1)**.

Page 13

1. **(a)** (upper) epidermis **(1)**; **(b)** spongy layer / mesophyll **(1)**; **(c)** air space **(1)**.
2. **Roots:** anchor plant in soil / absorb water and minerals **(1)**
   Stem: supports leaves and flowers, transports substances up and down the plant **(1)**
   Leaf: organs of photosynthesis **(1)**
   Flower: reproductive organs, formation of seeds **(1)**
3. **Any three from:** dead cells without cytoplasm; no end walls; hollow lumen; continuous tubes – all adaptations allow efficient movement of water in columns. **(3)**
4. **(a) Any one from:** phloem have perforated end walls / xylem has no end wall; xylem have hard cell walls (contain lignin) / phloem have soft cell walls. **(1)**
   (b) Aphids extract / eat sugar **(1)**; sugar solution transported in phloem **(1)**.

Page 14

1. **(a)** $\frac{8}{43} \times 100 = 18.6\%$ **(1 mark for calculation, 1 mark for correct answer)**
   (b) B (cold moving air) **(1)**
   (c) Water column in xylem would move upwards / towards the leaves more quickly. **(1)**

Page 15

1. **(a) (i)** Scotland **(1)**
   (ii) 50 deaths per 100 000 (210 – 160) **(1)**
   (b) Men have higher death rates than women. **(1)**
2. Artery – 3 **(1)**; Capillaries in the body – 4 **(1)**; Vein – 1 **(1)**; Capillaries in the lungs – 2 **(1)**

Page 16

1. **(a)** 924.5 **(2)**; **if the answer is incorrect then showing the working (926 + 923 = 1849, then $\frac{1849}{2}$) will gain 1 mark**
   (b) Rats have different body masses / to standardise results. **(1)**
   (c) As the warfarin dose increases, the time to clot also increases. **(1)**
2. Agree **(1)** because as vital capacity increases the time underwater also increases **(1)**.
   Or disagree **(1)** due to **any one from**: only five subjects / not enough data; need to find divers with higher / lower vital capacities **(1)**.

Page 17

1. **(a)** Light **(1)**
   (b) Accept one from: a negative result; no colour change; remains an orange/brown colour **(1)**
   (c) Repeat the investigation. **(1)**
   (d) An uncovered leaf. **(1)**
2. **(a)** Leaves **(1)**
   (b) Cellulose: cell walls for support **(1)**; **Protein:** growth / cell membranes / enzyme production **(1)**.
3. **(a)** It absorbs (sun)light. **(1)**
   (b) Limiting factor is a variable / parameter that restricts the rate of the photosynthesis / reaction **(1)**; **Accept one example:** temperature; amount of chlorophyll; carbon dioxide concentration **(1)**

HEALTH, DISEASE AND THE DEVELOPMENT OF MEDICINES

Page 18

1. **(a)** 13.8–14.8% **(1)**
   (b) Glycogen **(1)** found in liver / muscles **(1)**
   (c) Any two from: heart disease / CVD / stroke; cancer; diabetes; asthma / eczema / autoimmune diseases; poor nutrition – named example, e.g. rickets; genetic conditions, e.g. cystic fibrosis; eating disorders, e.g. anorexia; mental health conditions; alcoholism / addiction; named inherited disease. **(2)**
2. **(a)** ×20 **(1)**
   (b) Any one from: low birth weight; premature birth; higher risk of still birth. **(1)**

Page 19

1. **(a)** Pathogen **(1)**
   (b) Cause cell damage **(1)**; the toxins produced damage tissues. **(1)**
2. **(a) Any two from:** malaria is transmitted by the mosquito; warm temperatures are ideal for mosquitos to thrive; stagnant water is an ideal habitat for mosquito eggs to be laid / larvae to survive **(2)**.
   (b) Mosquito: vector **(1)**
   Plasmodium: parasite **(1)**
   (c) Nets will deter mosquitoes / prevent bites / prevent transferral of plasmodium **(1)**; antivirals are ineffective as plasmodium is a protist / not a virus **(1)**.

Page 20

1. **(a)** Antibodies **(1)**
   (b) Pathogens are clumped together to prevent their further reproduction, to make them easier for phagocytes to digest. **(1)**
   (c)

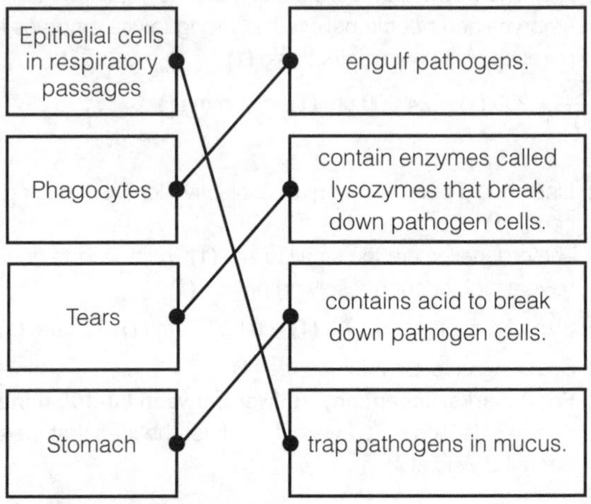

(1 mark for each correct line up to 3 marks, subtract 1 mark for any additional lines)

2. **(a) Any one from:** droplet infection / coughing / sneezing / water droplets in breath / aerosol. **(1)**
   (b) Answer in the range 16–17 days **(1)**
   (c) 9 arbitrary units **(1)** (9.5 – 0.5) **(1)**
   (d) Memory cells recognise future invasion of pathogen **(1)**; they can produce the necessary antibodies much quicker, and at higher levels, if the same pathogen is detected again **(1)**.

Page 21

1. **This is a model answer that would score the full 6 marks.** A vaccine contains weakened or attenuated pathogens, usually produced by heat treatment. When these foreign cells are injected into the body, antigens on their cell surface membrane are recognised as non-self by lymphocytes – a type of white blood cell. The lymphocytes then start to produce specific antibodies against the pathogen. As the pathogens are harmless, the body suffers no harm and memory cells are produced that remain in the body for years after. Each antigen in the vaccination will produce different antibodies specific to that disease.
2. **Accept any three from:** Bacteria are becoming resistant to many modern antibiotics; doctors have in the past over-prescribed antibiotics; mutations in bacteria have led to resistant strains developing; some people don't complete the course of antibiotics. **(3)**

Page 22

1. **(a) Any two from:** to ensure that the drug is actually effective / more effective than placebo; to work out the most effective dose / method of application; to comply with legislation. **(2)**
   (b) Double blind trials involve volunteers who are randomly allocated to groups – neither they nor the doctors / scientists know if they have been given the new drug or a placebo **(1)**; this eliminates all bias from the test **(1)**.
   (c) (i) Total patients = 226; $\frac{21}{226} \times 100$ **(1)** = 9.29% **(1)**
   (ii) Yes, there are more patients who took the drug and had a cardiovascular event than those who took the placebo. However, there is not a large difference between the groups. **(1)** No, the cardiovascular events could include other conditions apart from heart attacks. **(1)**
   (iii) Rash **(1)**; the difference in numbers of patients who got a rash between the alketronol and placebo groups is quite large **(1)**.

COORDINATION AND CONTROL

Page 23

1. homeostasis **(1)**; receptors **(1)**; effectors **(1)**
2. **(a)** Brain **(1)**
   (b) A means of detecting external stimuli, i.e. a **receptor (1)**; transferral of electrical impulses to the CNS, i.e. a **sensory neurone (1)**; a coordinator / control system, i.e. a **brain (1)**.

Page 24

1. **Gland:** pancreas **(1)** **Hormone:** insulin / glucagon **(1)**
2. **(a) Any two from:** after meal, a rise in glucose levels will be detected by device; which will cause hormone implant to release insulin; insulin released to bring blood glucose level down. **(2)**
   (b) People with type 2 diabetes can often control their sugar level by adjusting their diet **(1)**; body's cells often no longer respond to insulin **(1)**.
3.

Gland	Hormones produced
Pituitary gland	**TSH, ADH, LH** and **FSH (accept any two)**
Pancreas	Insulin and glucagon
Thyroid gland	Thyroxine
Adrenal gland	Adrenaline
Ovary	**Oestrogen** and **progesterone**
Testes	Testosterone

(1 mark for each correct line)

Page 25

1. Days 5–14: uterus wall is being repaired **(1)**; egg released at approximately 14 days from ovary **(1)**; days 14–28: uterus lining maintained **(1)**.
2.

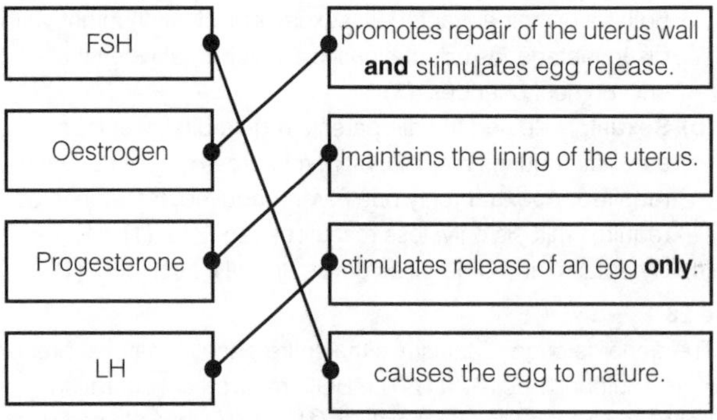

(1 mark for each correct line up to 3 marks)

3. **Girls: Accept any one change and reason from:** Breast growth – for production of milk to feed baby; Widening of hips – to accommodate gestating foetus; Growth of pubic and armpit hair – to attract the opposite sex. **(2)**
   Boys: Accept any one change and reason from: Production of sperm in testes – to fuse with an egg at fertilisation; Deepening of the voice/growth of pubic, facial and body hair – to attract the opposite sex. **(2)**

Page 26

1. **(a)**

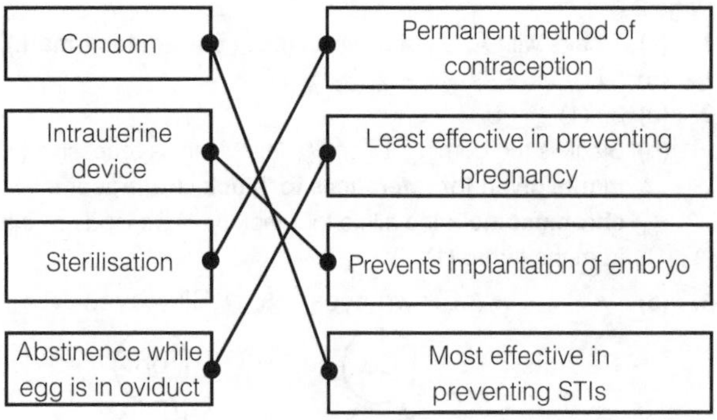

(1 mark for each correct line. If more than 3 lines drawn, subtract 1 mark for every extra line.)

   (b) Condom / diaphragm / IUD **(1)**; **Reason, accept any two from:** give high rates of protection against unwanted pregnancy; no side effects; not permanent (so can still have children). **(2)**
2. **Any two from:** the contraceptive pill contains hormones that inhibit FSH production; e.g. oestrogen / progesterone; eggs therefore fail to mature; progesterone causes production of sticky cervical mucus that hinders movement of sperm **(2)**.

INHERITANCE, VARIATION AND EVOLUTION

Page 27

1. gametes **(1)**; haploid **(1)**; meiosis **(1)**
2. Meiosis shuffles genes, which makes each gamete unique ✓ **(1)**; Gametes fuse randomly ✓ **(1)**

3. (a) **Any three from:** sexual reproduction can be an advantage to a species if the environment changes; asexual reproduction is more advantageous when the environment is not changing; some organisms use both types of reproduction, therefore both have their advantages; sexual reproduction might yield disadvantageous adaptations in an individual when the environment changes. **(3)**
   (b) **Sexual:** male and female parents required; slower than asexual; requires meiosis; more resources (e.g. time, energy) required. **Asexual:** only one parent required; faster than sexual; requires mitosis only; less resources required. **(1)**
   (c) Cytoplasm and organelles duplicated **(1)**; as a 'bud' **(1)**

Page 28

1. The genome of an organism is the entire genetic material present in its adult body cells ✓ **(1)**; The HGP involved collaboration between US and UK geneticists ✓ **(1)**; The project allowed genetic abnormalities to be tracked between generations ✓ **(1)**.
2. (a) Organisms with very similar features / chimpanzee and human share equal DNA coding for protein A. **(1)**
   (b) Yeast **(1)**
3. (a) **Any two from:** warn women about the risk of cancer ahead of time; enable early and regular screening; enable early treatment; suggest treatment that is targeted. **(2)**
   (b) Other factors may contribute to onset of cancer **(1)**; risk is in terms of a probability (which is not 100%) **(1)**.

Page 29

1. (a) T pairs with A; C pairs with G **(both correct for 1 mark)**
   (b) 3 **(1)**
2. (a) 39 **(1)**
   (b) Black is the dominant gene / allele; white is recessive **(1)** **(no marks given for references to 'black chromosome' or 'white chromosome')**; the allele for black fur is passed on / inherited from the father **(1)**.
3. (a)

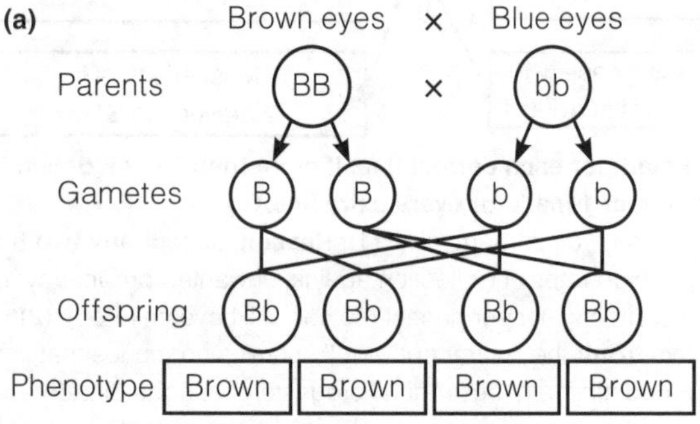

(1 mark will be awarded for the phenotype row and 1 mark for offspring row.)

   (b)

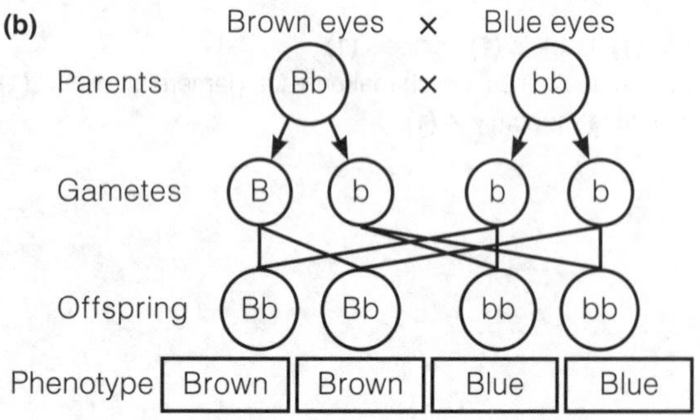

(1 mark will be awarded for the phenotype row and 1 mark for the offspring row.)

Page 30

1. (a) 205–215 million years ago **(1)**
   (b) (i) Cretaceous **(1)**
   (ii) They have discovered fossils. **(1)**
   (c) Lizard **(1)**
   (d) Archosaur **(1)**

Page 31

1. (a)

Before Industrial Revolution		After Industrial Revolution	
Pale	**Dark**	**Pale**	**Dark**
1260	107	89	1130

(1 mark for mean numbers before Industrial Revolution; 1 mark for mean numbers after Industrial Revolution)

   (b)

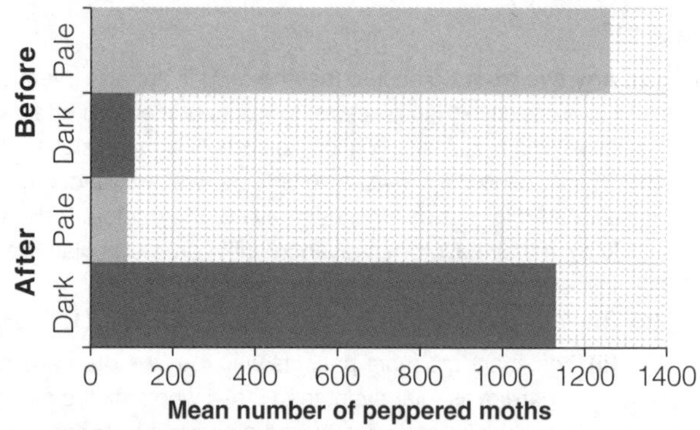

(2 marks for correct plotting of bars; subtract 1 mark for every incorrect plot.)

   (c) The pale-coloured moths could camouflage themselves easily against the silver birch tree bark. **(1)**
   (d) Dark-coloured peppered moths were more camouflaged than pale moths after the Industrial Revolution due to the effects of air pollution **(1)**; dark moths had an increased chance of survival and consequently an increased chance of reproducing and passing on genes **(1)**.

Page 32

1. (a) **Any three from:** Allow chosen males and females to mate / breed / reproduce together; select offspring from several matings that have high quality wool; allow these sheep to mate together; repeat the process over many generations **(stages must be in sequence)**. **(3)**
   (b) **Any one from:** high quality meat / lamb; thick coat; hardiness / ability to withstand harsh winters; colouration / markings; disease resistance. **(1)**

Page 33

1. **Any two from:** involves genes, not whole organisms; genes transferred from one organism to another; much more precise in terms of passing on characteristics; rapid production; cheaper than selective breeding; (or reverse argument). **(2)**
2. (a) Crops containing soya can be sprayed with herbicide so weeds are killed rather than soya. **(1)**
   (b) Rice produces carotene, which provides poor populations with vitamin A. **(1)**
3. GM plants may cross-breed with wild plants, resulting in wild plants / weeds that are herbicide-resistant. **(1)**

Page 34

1. (a) **Underline any one of the following**; carnivorous big cats; five toes on their front paws and four toes on their back paws; claws can be drawn back. **(1)**
   (b) Leopards are more closely related to tigers **(1)**; both are the Panthera genus / snow leopards are a different genus **(1)**.
2. Possesses features that are found in reptiles and birds **(1)**; feathers place it with birds but it also has teeth / does not have a beak like reptiles – it is an intermediate form **(1)**.

ECOSYSTEMS

Page 35

1. features; characteristics **(either way round for features or characteristics)**; suited; environment; evolutionary; survival **(6 words correct = 3 marks, 4 or 5 words correct = 2 marks, 2 or 3 words correct = 1 mark, 1 or 0 words correct = 0 marks)**
2. **(a)**

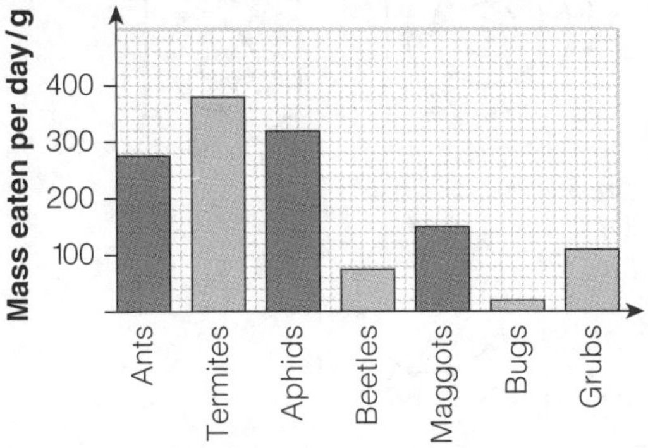

(2 marks for correctly plotting bars, 1 mark for correctly labelling x axis.)

(b) $\frac{380}{1330} \times 100 = 28.6\%$

(1 mark for correct answer, 1 mark for showing working)

(c) It occupies more than one habitat / niche **(1)**; eats a wide variety of food / prey **(1)**.

Page 36

1. **(a)** Habitat **(1)**
   (b) Ecosystem **(1)**
   (c) **Any one from:** pooter; sweepnet; light trap. **(1)**
   (d) 16 × 4 × 5000 = 320 000 **(1 mark for correct answer, 1 mark for showing working)**
   (e) **(i)** Less competition for food between beetles **(1)**; numbers increase as a result **(1)**.
   (ii) Snail numbers would decline. **(1)**

Page 37

1. **(a)** A producer is an organism that produces its own food. **(1)**
   (b) Sunlight / the Sun **(1)**
   (c) **Any one from:** wasp; ladybird; hoverfly **(1)**
2. **(a)** There was a slight rise in 1974 **(1)**, but since then the numbers have decreased rapidly **(1)**, and then they have decreased slowly **(1)**. The numbers decreased rapidly between 1976 and 1986 and decreased slowly between 1986 and 2002 **(1)**.
   (b) Farmers have cut down hedgerows and/or trees, so the birds have had nowhere to nest and their food source has been reduced. **(1)**
   (c) **Any one from:** plant more trees; encourage farmers to plant hedgerows; encourage farmers to leave field edges wild as food for birds; use fewer pesticides. **(1)**

Page 38

1. water wind wood **(1)**
2. **Climate zones** shift, causing ecosystems and habitats to change; organisms are displaced and become extinct. **(1) Sea levels** rise, causing flooding of coastal regions; islands are inundated and disappear beneath sea level. **(1) Ice caps and glaciers** melt and retreat, resulting in loss of habitat. **(1)**

Page 39

1. **Any two from:** climate change; new predators; habitat destruction; hunting; competition; pollution. **(2)**
2. **(a)** Cutting down large areas of forest ✓ **(1)**
   (b) Increase in atmospheric carbon dioxide ✓ **(1)**
3. **Any two from:** provide land for agriculture; road building; mining; construction. **(2)**
4. tropical; trees; carbon dioxide; biodiversity; extinct; habitats **(6)**
5. Nutrients in the soil are absorbed by crops and are not replaced. **(1)**

Page 40

1. organisms **(1)**, evaporated **(1)**, precipitation **(1)**
2. **(a)** Tube D **(1)**; because it is warm and moist **(1)**.
   (b) The soil / air / surface of the leaf **(1)**
   (c) So that air / oxygen can get in **(1)**
   (d) **Accept one from:** they could count the number of whole discs left at the end; they could record what fraction / percentage of leaf discs decayed and find an average; they could measure the percentage decrease in mass of discs by measuring mass before and after time in soil. **(1)**

Chemistry

ATOMIC STRUCTURE AND THE PERIODIC TABLE

Page 41

1. **(a)** Na **(1)** Cl **(1)**
   (b) sodium + chlorine ⟶ sodium chloride **(reactants 1, products 1)**
   (c) A compound **(1)** as the elements are chemically combined/joined **(1)**
   (d) A mixture **(1)** as the salt and water are together but not chemically combined **(1)**
   (e) Crystallisation **(1)**; simple distillation **(1)**

Page 42

1. **(a)** The plum pudding model proposed that an atom was a ball of positive charge/today's model has the positive charge contained in the nucleus/protons **(1)** The plum pudding model proposed that electrons were embedded/spread throughout the positive charge/today's model has the electrons in different energy levels/shells surrounding the positive charge **(1)**
   (b) Some of the positively charged particles/alpha particles (when fired at gold foil) were deflected **(1)**
   (c) Niels Bohr suggested that electrons orbit the nucleus at specific distances/are present in energy levels/shells **(1)** His calculations were backed up by experimental results **(1)**
   (d)

Particle	Relative charge	Relative mass
Proton	+1	**1**
Neutron	**0**	1
Electron	**–1**	**Very small/ approx. 1/2000**

(4)

   (e) **(i)** 11 **(1)**
   (ii) 23 **(1)**

Page 43

1. **(a)** 3 **(1)**
   (b) 2,7 **(1)**
   (c) 7 **(1)** As an atom of fluorine has 7 electrons in its outer shell **(1)**
2. **(a)** By increasing atomic number **(1)**
   (b) Because they both have similar chemical properties **(1)**
   (c) **Accept two from:** have high melting/boiling points; conduct heat and electricity; react with oxygen to form alkalis; malleable/ductile **(2)**

Page 44

1. **(a)** The atoms have full outer shells/energy levels **(1)** so they do not bond **(1)**
   (b) It increases **(1)**
2. **(a)** $2Na_{(s)} + 2H_2O_{(l)} \longrightarrow 2NaOH_{(aq)} + H_{2(g)}$ **(1 for correct formula; 1 for correct balancing in equation. Ignore state symbols, even if wrong)**
   (b) Blue **(1)** as an alkali solution/the hydroxide ion is formed **(1)**
   (c) A potassium atom is larger (than a sodium atom), so the outer electron is further away from the nucleus **(1)** so there is less attraction/the electron is more easily lost **(1)**
3. **(a)** $2Na_{(s)} + Cl_{(g)} \longrightarrow 2NaCl_{(s)}$ **(1 for each side; any correctly balanced equation scores both marks, e.g. $4Na + 2Br_2 \longrightarrow 4NaBr$)**
   (b) Ionic **(1)**
   (c) chlorine + sodium bromide ⟶ sodium chloride **(1)** + bromine **(1)**
   (d) Displacement **(1)** A more reactive element (chlorine) takes the place of a less reactive element (bromine) in a compound **(1)**

STRUCTURE, BONDING AND THE PROPERTIES OF MATTER

Page 45

1. sodium – metallic **(1)**; chlorine – simple molecular **(1)**; sodium chloride – ionic **(1)**
2. **(a)**

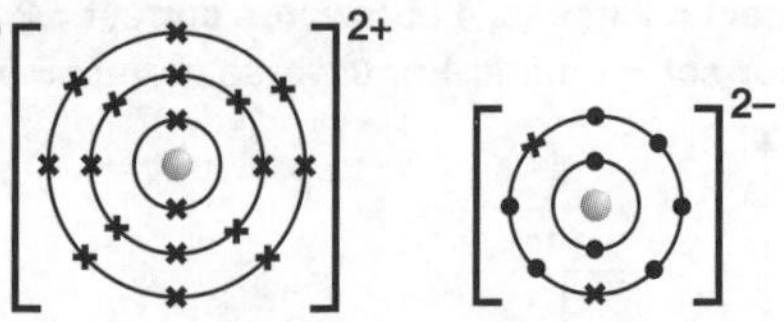

Ca^{2+} ion [2,8,8] O^{2-} ion [2,8] **(2)**

   (b) Calcium: 2+, oxygen: 2– **(2)**
3. **(a)**

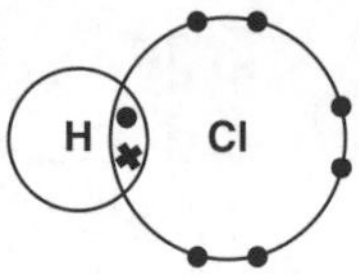

(1)

   (b) 2 **(1)**

Page 46

1. **(a)** Electrostatic forces **(1)** between the anions and cations
   (b) CaO **(1)** There are an equal number of calcium ions and oxygen ions and so the ratio of each is 1:1 **(1)**
2. **(a)** A polymer **(1)**
   (b) CH_2 **(1)** There are twice as many hydrogen atoms as carbon atoms, so ratio of carbon to hydrogen is 1:2 **(1)**
3. Giant covalent/macromolecular **(1)** it is a large molecule consisting of atoms that are covalently bonded together with a theoretically infinite structure **(1)**

Page 47

1. **(a)**

(1 for regular arrangement of particles, 1 for no gaps between the particles)

   (b) Intermolecular forces/forces between particles **(1)**
2. **(a)** It conducts electricity when liquid but not as a solid **(1)**
   (b) The ions **(1)** are not free to move **(1)**
   (c) Giant covalent/macromolecular **(1)** It has a high melting point and does not conduct electricity **(1)**
   (d) There are no free **(1)** charged particles/electrons/ions **(1)**

Page 48

1. **(a)** The layers **(1)** (of ions) are able to slide over each other **(1)**
   (b) There is a strong attraction **(1)** between the metal cations and the delocalised electrons **(1)**
   (c) The electrons **(1)** are free to move/flow through the structure **(1)**
2. **(a)** A mixture of metals/a metal mixed with another element **(1)**
   (b) The layers are not able to slide over each other **(1)** because the other atoms are larger and prevent movement **(1)**
3. **(a)** **Accept two from:** for drug delivery into the body/as lubricants/reinforcing materials, e.g. in tennis rackets **(2)**
   (b) **Accept two from:** tensile strength; electrical conductivity; thermal conductivity **(2)**
   (c) A carbon nanotube is a cylindrical fullerene **(1)**

QUANTITATIVE CHEMISTRY

Page 49

1. **(a)** Total mass of reactants = total mass of the products, i.e. there is no net mass loss or gain during a chemical reaction **(1)**
   (b)

Substance	A_r / M_r
Al	**27**
Fe_2O_3	**160**
Al_2O_3	**102**
Fe	**56**

(4)

2. **(a)** Oxygen **(1)** is added **(1)** to the magnesium
(b) $2Mg_{(s)} + O_{2(g)} \longrightarrow 2MgO_{(s)}$ **(1 for reactants and products, 1 for correct balancing)**
(c) The magnesium carbonate loses/gives off **(1)** carbon dioxide **(1)**
(d) $MgCO_{3(s)} \longrightarrow MgO_{(s)} + CO_{2(g)}$ **(1 for correct formulae products; 1 for balanced equation; ignore state symbols, even if wrong)**

Page 50

1. **(a)** +/– 0.005 g (i.e. half of the uncertainty) **(1)**
(b) 24.5 cm^3 and 25.5 cm^3. **(1)** The uncertainty is half the scale division (i.e. half of 1 cm^3) or +/– 0.5 cm^3. Therefore the volume lies between 25 cm^3 – 0.5 cm^3 = 24.5 cm^3 and 25 cm^3 + 0.5 cm^3 = 25.5 cm^3 **(1)**
2. **(a)** A solid that is dissolved in a liquid to form a solution. **(1)**
(b) (45 ÷ 1000) x 600 = 27g **(1)**
(c) (12 ÷ 225) x 1000 = 53 **(1)**
(d) Solution B **(1)**. It has a higher concentration **(1)**.

CHEMICAL AND ENERGY CHANGES

Page 51

1. **(a)** calcium + oxygen ⟶ calcium oxide **(1 for reactants, 1 for product)**
(b) Calcium gains **(1)** oxygen **(1)** (**Also accept** Oxygen **(1)** is added **(1)** **or** Calcium loses **(1)** electrons **(1)**)
(c) Potassium, sodium or lithium (or any other metal in group 1 or strontium, barium or radium) **(1)** the metal is more reactive than calcium/is above calcium in the reactivity series **(1)**
(d) metal + calcium oxide ⟶ metal oxide + calcium, e.g. potassium + calcium oxide ⟶ potassium oxide + calcium **(1 for reactants, 1 for products)**
(e) Calcium oxide **(1)**
2. **(a)** Electrolysis **(1)**
(b) $2Fe_2O_3 + 3C \longrightarrow 4Fe + 3CO_2$ **(1 for correct formulae, 1 for balanced equation; allow any correct balanced equation, e.g. $4Fe_2O_3 + 6C \longrightarrow 8Fe + 6CO_2$ ignore state symbols)**
(c) Aluminium is higher in the reactivity series **(1)** than carbon **(1)**
(d) aluminium oxide **(1)** because it loses oxygen **(1)**

Page 52

1. **(a)** Zinc sulfate **(1)**
(b) zinc oxide + hydrochloric acid ⟶ zinc chloride **(1)** + water **(1)**
(c) effervescence or fizzing / bubbling **(1)**; the zinc carbonate / solid dissolves **(1)**
(d) Carbon dioxide **(1)** CO_2 **(1)**
(e) No gas is produced in the reaction **(1)**
2. **(a)** **Accept three from:** measure out some sulfuric acid (e.g. 25 cm^3 in a measuring cylinder); transfer to a beaker and warm the acid; add copper oxide, stir and repeat until no more copper oxide dissolves; filter the mixture; leave the filtrate somewhere warm/heat the filtrate **(3)**
(b) Nitric acid **(1)**

Page 53

1. **(a)** 1–6 **(1)**
(b) Hydrogen ion **(1)** H^+ **(1)**
(c) Hydrochloric acid **(1)**
(d) $H^+_{(aq)} + OH^-_{(aq)} \longrightarrow H_2O_{(l)}$ **(1 for correct formulae, 1 for correct state symbols)**
(e) Pink **(1)**
2. Cation – A positive ion **(1)**
Anion – A negative ion **(1)**
Anode – The positive electrode **(1)**
Cathode – The negative electrode **(1)**
Electrolysis – The separating of chemicals using electricity **(1)**
Electrolyte – The liquid or solution containing ions that is broken down during electrolysis **(1)**

Page 54

1. **(a)** Cations **(1)**
(b) Anions **(1)**
(c) So that the ions **(1)** are free to move **(1)**
2. **(a)**

Solution	Product at anode	Product at cathode
NaCl	H_2	$\mathbf{Cl_2}$
KNO_3	$\mathbf{H_2}$	$\mathbf{O_2}$
$CuSO_4$	**Cu**	$\mathbf{O_2}$
Water diluted with sulfuric acid	$\mathbf{H_2}$	O_2

(6)

(b) Hydrogen is produced because hydrogen ions are present in the solution **(1)** and hydrogen is less reactive than sodium **(1)**

Page 55

1. **(a)** 2.5°C **(1)**
(b) Endothermic **(1)** because the temperature decreases **(1)**
(c) It increases **(1)**
2. **(a)**

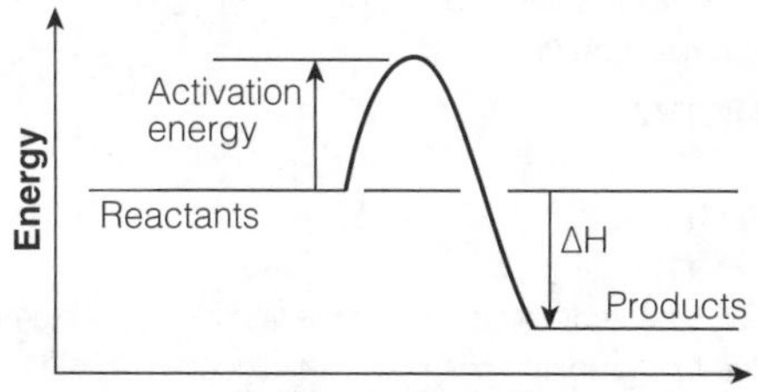

(1 for products lower in energy than the reactants, each correct label scores 1)
(b) **Accept one from:** any thermal decomposition reaction (e.g. metal carbonate ⟶ metal oxide + carbon dioxide); The reaction between citric acid and sodium hydrogencarbonate **(1)**

THE RATE AND EXTENT OF CHEMICAL REACTIONS

Page 56

1. **(a)** 70°C **(1)**
(b) Increased temperature increases the rate of reaction **(1)** the higher the temperature, the more kinetic energy the particles have and so the frequency of collisions/successful collisions increases **(1)**
2. **(a)** 1st experiment: 69 ÷ 46 = 1.5 **(1)** cm^3/s; 2nd experiment: 18 ÷ 10 = 1.8 **(1)** cm^3/s **(1 for correct units)**
(b) The second experiment **(1)** as the rate is greater **(1)**

Page 57

1. **(a)**

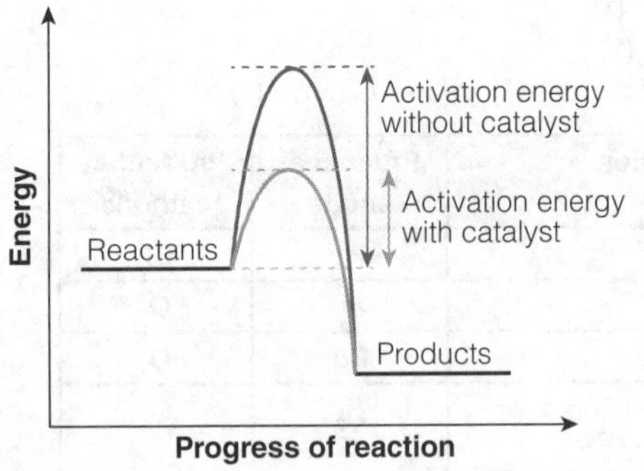

(1)

(b) Catalysts provide an alternative reaction pathway **(1)** of lower activation energy **(1)**

2. **(a)** The blue crystals will turn white **(1)**
(b) hydrated copper(II) sulfate $\rightleftharpoons$ anhydrous copper(II) sulfate + water **(allow arrow $\longrightarrow$ instead of $\rightleftharpoons$) (1 for formulae, 1 for balanced equation)**
(c) The white powder will turn blue **(1)**
(d) Exothermic reaction **(1)**

ORGANIC CHEMISTRY

Page 58

1. **(a)** Kerosene **(1)**
(b) It increases **(1)**
(c) 1. Crude oil is heated/boiled **(1)** 2. In the fractionating column there is a temperature gradient (hotter at bottom/cooler at top) **(1)** 3. The hydrocarbons travel up the fractionating column and condense at their boiling point **(1)**

2. **(a)** C_nH_{2n+2} **(1)**
(b)

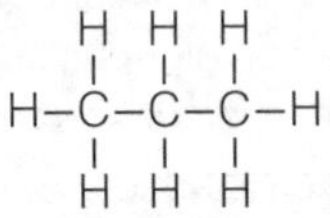

(1)

(c) C_4H_{10} **(1)**
(d) **Any one from:** differ by CH_2 in their molecular formula from neighbouring compounds; show a gradual trend in physical properties; have similar chemical properties **(1)**

Page 59

1. **(a)** carbon dioxide **(1)** and water **(1)**
(b) $C_3H_8 + 5O_2 \longrightarrow 3CO_2 + 4H_2O$ **(1 mark for correct formulae and 1 mark for correct balancing)**
(c) propane **(1)**

2. **(a)** **Accept one from:** silica, alumina, porcelain **(1)**
(b) by heating **(1)** with steam **(1)**
(c) C_4H_{10} **(1)**
(d) Bromine water **(1)** turns colourless / is decolourised / turns from orange to colourless when mixed with the gas **(1)**

CHEMICAL ANALYSIS

Page 60

1. **(a)** A mixture that has been designed as a useful product **(1)**
(b) No **(1)** something that is chemically pure contains a single element or compound **(1)**
(c) **Accept one from:** fuels; medicines; foods; fertilisers **(1)**

2. **(a)** The liquid solvent **(1 allow water)**
(b) red and green **(1)** The spots of these colours are at the same height as spots in ink X **(1)**
(c) $\frac{0.5}{4.65} = 0.11$ **(allow 0.10–0.12; 1 mark for working, 1 mark for correct answer)**

Page 61

1. **(a)** Calcium hydroxide **(1)**
(b) A precipitate **(1)** of $CaCO_3$ **(1)** is formed

2. **(a)** The litmus paper turns red **(1)** before turning white/being bleached **(1)**
(b) Acidic gas **(1)** as it turns litmus paper red **(1)**

3. **(a)** Hydrogen gives a squeaky pop **(1)** when exposed to a lit splint **(1)**
(b) Oxygen relights **(1)** a glowing splint **(1)**
(c) $2H_{2(g)} + O_{2(g)} \longrightarrow 2H_2O_{(l)}$ **(1 for formulae of reactants/ products, 1 for correctly balanced equation; ignore state symbols)**

THE EARTH'S ATMOSPHERE AND RESOURCES

Page 62

1. **(a)** Nitrogen or oxygen **(1)**
(b) The water vapour originally in the atmosphere cooled **(1)** and condensed **(1)** forming the oceans
(c) Green plants/algae **(1)** form oxygen as a waste product of photosynthesis **(1)**
(d) **Accept two from:** green plants; algae use carbon dioxide for photosynthesis; carbon dioxide is used to form sedimentary rocks; carbon dioxide is captured in oil; coal **(2)**

Page 63

1. **(a)** Greenhouse gases allow short wavelength radiation from the Sun to pass through the atmosphere **(1)** but absorb long wavelength radiation reflected back from the earth trapping heat **(1)**
(b) **Accept one from:** methane; water vapour **(1)**
(c) **Accept two from:** combustion of fossil fuels; deforestation; increased animal farming; decomposing rubbish in landfill sites **(2)**
(d) There are many different factors contributing to climate change **(1)** and it is not easy to predict the impact of each one **(1)**
(e) **Accept two from:** rising sea levels, which may cause flooding and coastal erosion; more frequent and/or severe storms; changes to the amount, timing and distribution of rainfall; temperature and water stress for humans and wildlife; changes to the food-producing capacity of some regions/changes to the distribution of wildlife species **(2)**
(f) **Accept two from:** use of alternative energy supplies; increased use of renewable energy; energy conservation; carbon capture and storage techniques; carbon taxes and licences; carbon offsetting/carbon neutrality **(2)**
(g) **Accept two from:** disagreement over the causes and consequences of global climate change; lack of public information and education; lifestyle changes, e.g. greater use of cars and aeroplanes; economic considerations, i.e. the financial costs of reducing the carbon footprint; incomplete international co-operation **(2)**

Page 64

1. **(a)** Fuel formed in the ground over millions of years from the remains of dead plants and animals **(1)**
(b) Due to incomplete combustion/burning of fuels in a poor supply of oxygen **(1)**
(c) **Accept one from:** forms acid rain; can cause respiratory problems **(1)**
(d) Global dimming **(1)** health problems due to lung damage **(1)**
(e) It combines with haemoglobin/red blood cells **(1)** preventing the transport of oxygen **(1)**
(f) When sulfur burns it react with oxygen to form sulfur dioxide **(1)** Sulfur dioxide dissolves in rain water **(1)** The rain water is now acidic/acid rain which can damage buildings and destroy wildlife **(1)**

Page 65

1. **(a)** The needs of the current generation are met without compromising the potential of future generations to meet their own needs **(1)** Improving agricultural practices/using chemical processes to make new materials **(1)**
   (b) Water that is safe to drink **(1)**
   (c) Filtration/passed through filter beds to remove solid impurities **(1)** sterilised to kill microbes **(1)**
   (d) **Accept three from:** screening and grit removal; sedimentation to produce sewage sludge and effluent; anaerobic digestion of sewage sludge; aerobic biological treatment of effluent **(3)**
2. **(a)**

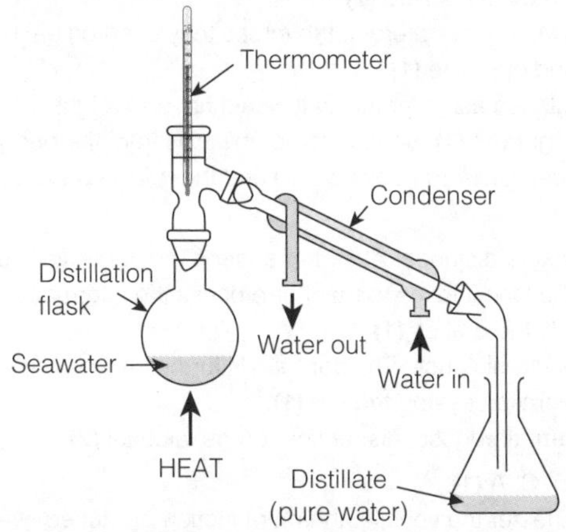

   (3 for labelled diagram: seawater in flask, condenser, pure water being collected)
   The water from the seawater boils/evaporates at 100°C and is condensed back into water in the condenser **(1)** the salt remains behind in the original flask **(1)**
   (b) Reverse osmosis **(1)**

Page 66

1. **(a)** **Accept two from:** extracting and processing raw materials; manufacturing and packaging; disposal at end of useful life **(2)**
   (b) **Accept two from:** how much energy is needed; how much water is used; what resources are required; how much waste is produced; how much pollution is produced **(2)**
   (c) Allocating numerical values to pollutant effects is not always easy or straightforward **(1)** so value judgments have to be made which may not always be objective **(1)**
   (d) To support claims for advertising purposes **(1)**
2. Over the life of the product, plastic bags when compared with paper bags (**accept two from the following**): use less energy; use less fossil fuel; produce fewer CO_2 emissions; produce less waste; use less freshwater **(2)** meaning that plastic/polythene bags are less damaging to the environment/have less of an environmental impact **(1)** than paper bags **(Allow reverse argument)**

Physics

FORCES

Page 67

1. **(a)** weight = mass × gravitational field strength
   78 × 10 = 780 N **(1)**
   (b) Mass would be 78 kg (the same as on Earth) **(1)**.
   weight = mass × gravitational field strength
   78 × 1.6 = 124.8 N **(1)**
   (c) The gravitational attraction of Neil is very small **(1)**. The masses of the Moon and Earth are much larger than Neil so the gravitational attraction has no significant effect on them **(1)**.
2. **(a)** 120 – 30 **(1)** = 90 N **(1)**
   (b) **(i)** 0 N **(1)**
   (ii) Louise is moving at a constant speed **(1)**. As the resultant force is zero she is neither accelerating nor decelerating **(1)**.
   (c) $\frac{\text{work done}}{\text{force}} = \text{distance moved along the line of action of the force}$
   $= \frac{25\,000}{90}$ **(1)** = 278 m **(1)**

Page 68

1. **(a)** Linear **(1)**
   (b) force = spring constant × extension
   spring constant = $\frac{\text{force}}{\text{extension}}$ **(1)**
   $\frac{4}{0.01}$ – substitute numbers from graph **(1)**
   = 400 N/m **(1)**
   (c) **(i)** Non-linear
   (ii) The mass is too large **(1)** so the spring has exceeded the limit of proportionality **(1)**. The extension is no longer proportional to the force applied **(1)**.

Page 69

1. **(a)** Speed only has a magnitude **(1)**. Velocity has a magnitude and a direction **(1)**.
   (b) 1.5 m/s – Walking
   6 m/s – Bicycle
   20 m/s – Car
   250 m/s – Plane **(4 marks if fully correct; 1 mark per match)**
2. **(a)** speed = $\frac{\text{distance}}{\text{time}}$ **(1)** = $\frac{180}{13}$ = 14 m/s (2 s.f.) **(1)**
   (b) speed = $\frac{\text{distance}}{\text{time}}$ **(1)**
   time = $\frac{\text{distance}}{\text{speed}}$
   = $\frac{500}{14}$ = 36 seconds (2 s.f.) **(1)**

Page 70

1. **(a)** speed = $\frac{\text{distance}}{\text{time}}$ **(1)** = $\frac{3500}{350}$ = 10 m/s **(1)**
   (b) gradient = $\frac{1750}{50\text{ seconds}}$ **(1)** = 35 m/s **(1)**
2. **(a)** 250 – 300 seconds **(1)**
   (b) gradient = $\frac{100}{50}$ **(1)** = 2 m/s^2 **(1)**
3. A skydiver accelerates due to their weight **(1)** exceeding the air resistance **(1)**. As they reach terminal velocity **(1)** their weight balances the air resistance, or the resultant force is zero, so they stop accelerating and maintain a constant speed **(1)**.

Page 71

1. **(a)** **(i)** A stationary object will begin moving and accelerate **(1)**.
   (ii) A moving object will either accelerate or decelerate **(1)**.
   (b) Newton's first law **(1)**
2. **(a)** The acceleration of an object is proportional to the resultant force **(1)**.
   (b) **(i)** resultant force = mass × acceleration **(1)**
   = 110 × 5
   = 550 N **(1)**
   (ii) The resultant forces are unbalanced **(1)**. The force opposing the cyclist's movement is greater than the force of the cyclist's movement **(1)**. When she stops the resultant force on her is zero **(1)**.
3. Whenever two objects interact, the forces they exert on each other are equal and opposite **(1)**.
4. A vehicle with a mass over the limit would have a weight downwards greater **(1)** than the force upwards from the bridge **(1)**. There is a resultant force downwards and the bridge breaks **(1)**.

Page 72

1. **(a)** **(i)** Thinking distance: At higher speeds the car travels further in the time it takes to react or process the information and apply the brakes **(1)**.
   (ii) Braking distance: The car travels further in the time it takes the brakes to stop the car **(1)**.
   (b) **Two from:** tiredness; distraction; drugs; alcohol **(2)**
   (c) **(i)** B, D, C, A **(1)**
   (ii) The faster the vehicle, the more friction produced when brakes are applied / more work done **(1)**. This causes the brakes to heat up to a higher temperature **(1)**.
   (iii) The temperatures would increases **(1)** but the results will still follow the same pattern **(1)**.

ENERGY

Page 73

1. **(a)** g.p.e. = mass × gravitational field strength × height **(1)**
   = 60 × 10 × 3900
   = 2 340 000 J or 2340 kJ **(1)**
   (b) kinetic energy = 0.5 × mass × $(\text{speed})^2$ **(1)**
   = 0.5 × 60 × 55^2
   = 90 750 J / 90.75 kJ **(1)**
   (c) kinetic energy = 0.5 × mass × $(\text{speed})^2$ **(1)**
   = 0.5 × 60 × 5^2
   = 750 J **(1)**
   (d) 0 J **(1)**
2. **(a)** Copper **(1)** as it has the lowest specific heat capacity. **(1)**
   (b) Temperature change = 35 – 16 = 19°C **(1)**
   $\frac{(\text{change in thermal energy} \div \text{temperature change})}{\text{specific heat capacity}} = \text{mass}$
   $= \frac{(76\,000 \div 19)}{390}$ **(1)**
   = 10 kg (2 s.f.) **(1)**

Page 74

1. transferred ✓ **(1)** dissipated ✓ **(1)**
2. **(a)** House B **(1)** has the lowest heating cost **(1)**. It is well insulated so loses less heat through the walls **(1)**.
   (b) No **(1)** not all heat is lost through walls **(1)**. Insulation in other areas could affect heating cost as could the efficiency of the boiler providing the heat **(1)**.
   (c) efficiency = $\frac{\text{useful output energy transfer}}{\text{useful input energy transfer}}$ **(1)**
   useful output energy transfer = efficiency × useful input energy transfer
   = 0.65 × 5400 = 3510 kJ **(1)**

Page 75

1. Renewable energy: **Three from**: solar; wind; wave; tidal; geothermal; hydroelectric
   Non-renewable energy: **Three from**: coal; oil; gas; nuclear
   (3 marks if fully correct; 2 marks if five correct; 1 mark if three correct)
2. **(a)** Over time the percentage of electricity generated by wind turbines has increased **(1)**.
   (b) Renewable energy so will not run out like fossil fuels **(1)**, doesn't release carbon dioxide or other pollutants **(1)**.
   (c) No **(1)**. Wind doesn't blow all the time **(1)** so we will always need another source of energy to provide 'back up' and supply electricity when wind turbines aren't turning **(1)**.
   (d) Some people think they are ugly and spoil views of landscapes **(1)**.

WAVES

Page 76

1. **(a)** A longitudinal wave **(1)**
   (b) wave speed = frequency × wavelength **(1)**
   $\text{wavelength} = \frac{\text{wave speed}}{\text{frequency}} = \frac{1482}{120} = 12.4$ metres **(1)**
   (c) Water is denser than air **(1)** so the sound wave is propagated faster **(1)**.
   (d) Water waves are transverse waves where the oscillations are perpendicular to the direction of energy transfer **(1)**. Sound waves are longitudinal waves where the oscillations are parallel to the direction of energy transfer **(1)**.
2. Amplitude – The maximum displacement of a point on a wave away from its undisturbed position. **(1)**
   Wavelength – The distance from a point on one wave to the equivalent point on the adjacent wave. **(1)**
   Frequency – The number of waves passing a point each second. **(1)**

Page 77

1. A: Radio **(1)** B: Infrared **(1)** C: Gamma **(1)**
2. **(a)** Changes in the nucleus of a radioactive atom **(1)**.
   (b) Sterilisation of equipment or other suitable answer **(1)**.
   (c) They can cause gene mutations **(1)** and cancer **(1)**.
3. Radiation dose **(1)**
4. 299792458 m/s **(1)**. Both visible light and X-rays are electromagnetic waves **(1)** so both travel at the same speed through the vacuum of space **(1)**.

ELECTRICITY AND MAGNETISM

Page 78

1. **(a)** fuse **(1)**
   (b) thermistor **(1)**
   (c) switch (closed) **(1)**
2. **(a)** X: Filament lamp **(1)**, Y: LED **(1)**, Z: Resistor **(1)**
   (b) 5A **(1)**
   (c) The flow of electrical charge **(1)**
   (d) charge flow = current × time **(1)**
   $\text{time} = \frac{\text{charge flow}}{\text{current}} = \frac{780}{5}$
   = 156 seconds **(1)**

Page 79

1. **(a)** Ohmic conductor **(1)**
   (b) Temperature **(1)**
   (c)

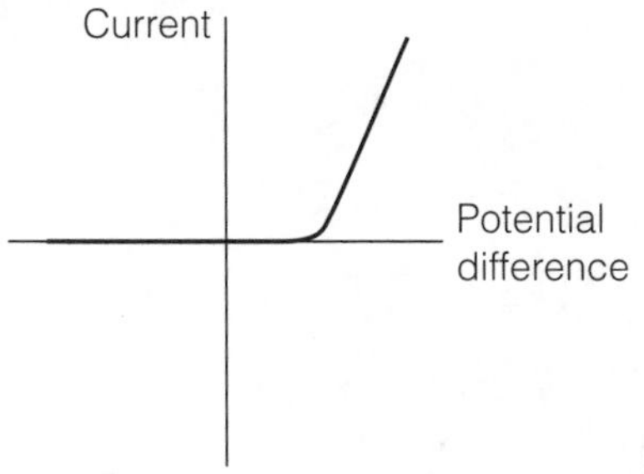

(2)

2. $\frac{\text{potential difference}}{\text{resistance}}$ = current **(1)** $= \frac{15}{4}$
   = 3.75 A **(1)**
3. The potential difference across a component and the current through it are required to calculate its resistance **(1)**. The ammeter is wired in parallel not in series so can't be used to measure the current **(1)**. The voltmeter is wired in series not in parallel so can't be used to measure the potential difference **(1)**.

Page 80

1. **(a)** A series circuit **(1)**
   (b) Total resistance = 4 + 5 + 2 **(1)**
   = 11Ω **(1)**
2. **(a)** 2A **(1)**
   (b) 8V **(1)**
   (c) $\text{resistance} = \frac{\text{potential difference}}{\text{current}} = \frac{8}{2}$
   = 4Ω **(1)**
   (d) The total resistance of all the components would be greater **(1)**. The total resistance of components wired in series is the sum of the individual resistors **(1)**. In parallel the total resistance is always lower than the resistance of an individual resistor **(1)**.

Page 81

1. Live wire – Brown – Carries the alternating potential difference from the supply.
   Neutral wire – Blue – Completes the circuit.
   Earth wire – Green and yellow stripes – Only carries a current if there is a fault.
   (3 marks if fully correct; 1 mark for each correct match of wire, colour and function)
2. **(a)** Alternating current **(1)**.The sander is plugged into the mains electricity which is a.c. **(1)**.
   (b) There is the risk of touching a live wire **(1)**. Our bodies are at earth potential (0 V) **(1)**. Touching a live wire would produce a large potential difference across a body. **(1)**. This would cause a current to flow through the body **(1)** resulting in an electric shock that could cause serious injury or death.
   (c) The potential difference of the mains supply is 230V **(1)**. The potential difference of the batteries is much lower / there is a reduced risk of harm **(1)**.

Page 82

1. **(a)** power = current^2 × resistance **(1)** = $3^2 \times 76.7$
   = 690.3 W **(1)**
   (b) Electrical **(1)** to kinetic and heat **(1)**.
   (c) energy transferred = power × time **(1)**
   $\text{time} = \frac{\text{energy transferred}}{\text{power}} = \frac{180\,000}{690.3} = 261$ seconds **(1)**
   (d) The potential difference is high in cables to reduce heat loss **(1)** and improve efficiency **(1)**. The potential difference is reduced in homes for safety **(1)**.

Page 83

1. **(a)** S **(1)**
   (b) N **(1)**
   (c) N **(1)**
2. **(a)** Magnetic field **(1)**
   (b) Attraction **(1)**
   (c) Force would be stronger at A than at B **(1)**. A is closer to the poles of the magnet / the magnetic field lines are closer together at A **(1)**.
3. The magnetic field around a solenoid is the same shape as the magnetic field around a bar magnet. ✓ **(1)**
   A solenoid with an iron core is an electromagnet. ✓ **(1)**

PARTICLE MODEL OF MATTER

Page 84

1. **(a)** density = $\frac{\text{mass}}{\text{volume}}$ **(1)**

   density = $\frac{5}{0.002}$

   = 2500 kg/m^3 **(1)**

   (b) The density would decrease **(1)** as gas was released **(1)**. The mass of the fire extinguisher would decrease but the volume would remain the same **(1)**.

2. **(a)** Differences in temperature would affect the pressure of the gas **(1)**.

   (b) Differences in volume would affect the pressure **(1)**.

3. **(a)** 3 kg of water **(1)**. Mass is conserved during changes of state **(1)**.

   (b) The change has been reversed and the ice has regained its original properties **(1)**. This occurs in physical changes but not in chemical changes **(1)**.

Page 85

1. **(a)** **(i)** 10°C **(1)** **(ii)** 60°C **(1)**

   (b) The temperature is staying the same **(1)** so it is changing state **(1)** and the stored internal energy is changing **(1)**.

   (c) energy for a change of state = mass × specific latent heat **(1)**

   = 0.5 × 250 000

   = 125 000 J **(1)** or 125 KJ

ATOMIC STRUCTURE

Page 86

1. **(a)** **(i)** 6 **(1)**

   (ii) 6 **(1)**

   (iii) 6 **(1)**

   (b) **(i)** Isotopes **(1)**

   (ii) They have different numbers of neutrons **(1)**.

2. **(a)** Nuclear model has a nucleus with electrons orbiting **(1)**. Plum pudding model suggested atom was a ball of positive charge with negative electrons embedded or scattered in it **(1)**.

   (b) It provided evidence of existence of neutrons **(1)**.

Page 87

1. **(a)** **(i)** A: Alpha **(1)**, B: Gamma **(1)**, C: Beta **(1)**

   (ii) Most to least: Alpha, Beta, Gamma **(2 marks if fully correct; 1 mark for two correct)**

2. **(a)** Alpha **(1)**

   (b) A: 92, B: 234, C: 4, D: 2 **(3 marks if fully correct; 2 marks for three correct; 1 mark for two correct)**

   (c) There is no effect on the mass or the charge of the nucleus **(1)**.

Page 88

1. contamination; decay; emit; Irradiation; radiation; radioactive **(3 marks if fully correct; 2 marks if one error; 1 mark if two errors)**

2. **(a)** **(i)** 20 days **(1)**

   (ii) This is the length of time it takes for the activity (counts per second) to halve **(1)**.

   (iii) Counts per second at 20 days = 250

   Counts per second at 40 days = $\frac{250}{2}$ = 125 **(1)**

   Counts per second at 60 days = $\frac{125}{2}$ = 62.5 **(1)**

Biology Paper 1 Foundation

Question number	Answer	Notes	Marks
01.1	cell, tissue, organ, system		1
01.2	Carbon dioxide		1
01.3	Starch – For storage Cellulose – To make cell walls Amino acids – For protein synthesis		2
01.4	During respiration all the energy required is released from the glucose made during photosynthesis		1 1
02.1	**A** = nucleus, **B** = cytoplasm, **C** = cell wall	1 mark for each correct answer	3
02.2	Cell wall		1
02.3	×400		1
02.4	A higher magnification means you can see the cells in much more detail, which means scientists can learn more about the structure of cells.		1 1
03.1	Lactic acid		1
03.2	Her muscles can release more energy.		1
03.3	**Cause:** build-up of lactic acid (in muscles) **Recovery:** heavy breathing / panting over a period of time		1 1 1
03.4	**Any three from:** More blood to the muscles. More oxygen supplied to muscles. Increased energy transfer in muscles. More lactic acid to be removed from muscles.		3
04.1	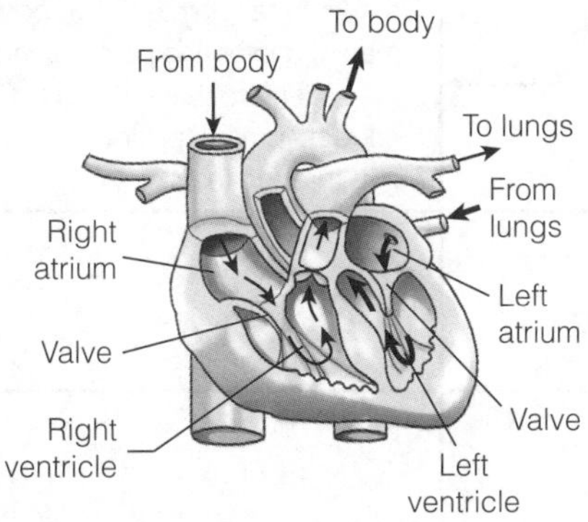	Award mark for arrows pointing in the correct direction.	1
04.2	Blood is pumped at a higher pressure. / Blood is pumped a greater distance.		1
04.3	They stop the backflow of blood.	Allow: they stop blood flowing in the wrong direction.	1
04.4	$\frac{22100}{105650} \times 100 = 20.91812\%$ 21% to two significant figures		1 1
04.5	**Any two from:** Low(er) fat intake Low(er) salt intake Regular exercise Healthy body weight Low stress levels		2
05.1	To stop evaporation (of the water)		1
05.2	2.5 cm^3 per day $\frac{50 - 40}{4}$	Allow 1 mark for: total volume lost = 10 cm^3	1 1
05.3	Used for photosynthesis Stops the plant from wilting **or** keeps the cells turgid		1 1

Question number	Answer	Notes	Marks
05.4	It is lost by evaporation through the stomata in the leaves into the air		1 1
05.5	As the percentage humidity increases, the rate of transpiration decreases. Higher humidity means more water in the air so it is harder for the plant to lose more water.		1 1 1
06.1	Amylase		1
06.2	Protease		1
06.3	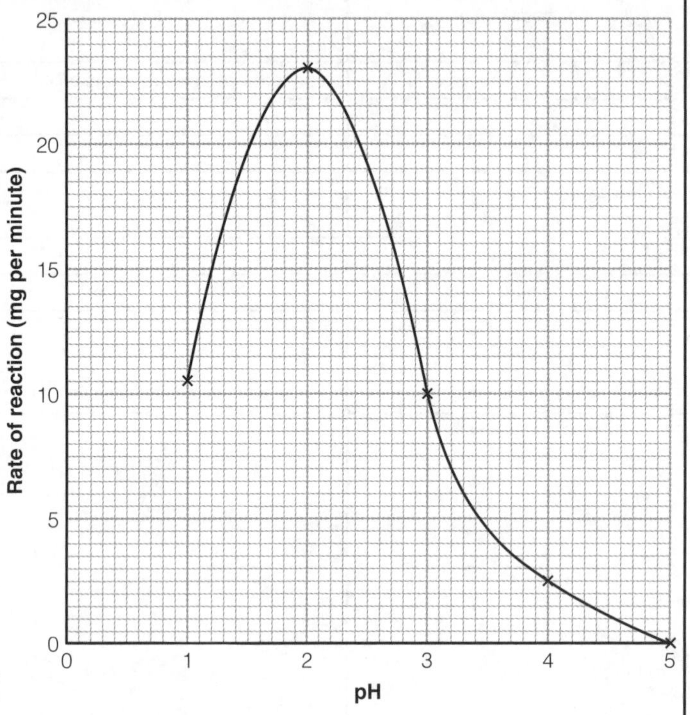	2 marks for all points drawn correctly; 1 mark if one or two points is incorrect; 0 marks if more than two points is incorrect; 1 mark for drawing a smooth curve through the points	3
06.4	At first, when the pH increases, the rate of formation of the product increases. The rate of formation of product reaches a maximum around pH 2 and then it decreases again until the reaction stops at pH 5.		1 1 1
06.5	**One from:** To get optimum enzyme activity pH affects the shape of the enzyme/changes enzyme activity		1
06.6	Enzymes are denatured at 60 °C. So proteins / fats from food are not broken down.		1 1
07.1	The movement of water particles across a partially permeable membrane		1
07.2	Water has moved / diffused into sugar solution from a dilute to a more concentrated solution. Visking tubing is partially permeable.		1 1 1
08.1	Higher temperature leads to faster growth. More carbon dioxide leads to faster growth.		1 1
08.2	Water oxygen		1 1

Question number	Answer	Notes	Marks
08.3	**Indicative content** **Patterns / predictions** • Fewer bubbles / less photosynthesis with increasing distance • More bubbles at 35 °C • Fewer / no bubbles at 55 °C • Rate of photosynthesis decreases with increasing distance • Rate of photosynthesis increases with temperature up to around 45 °C • Photosynthesis stops at higher temperature **Explanations** • Increase in distance reduces the amount of light • Less light, less photosynthesis • Higher temperature up to around 45 °C – more photosynthesis • More energy increases photosynthesis • Rate of photosynthesis decreases with decrease in light intensity • Correct mention of inverse square law • Rate of photosynthesis increases with increasing energy • Above 45 °C enzymes are denatured and so little or no photosynthesis	**Level 3:** Correct patterns for linking both temperature and distance to *rate* of photosynthesis. Explanations linked to light intensity, energy and enzymes. **Level 2:** One correct pattern / prediction outlined for both distance and temperature. One correct explanation linked to one pattern / prediction. **Level 1:** One correct pattern / prediction outlined for either distance or temperature. One correct explanation linked to the pattern / prediction. **Level 0:** No relevant content	5–6 3–4 1–2 0
09.1	**Any four from:** Sterilise wire / inoculate loop in flame. Transfer sample of pond water to agar. Seal lid with a cross of tape. Turn upside down (to stop condensation). Incubate at 25 °C.		4
09.2	I would use disinfectant C It is the most effective at killing the bacteria in the pond water because when compared to A and B it has a bigger area around it with no bacteria growing.		1 1 1

Biology Paper 2 Foundation

Question Number	Answer	Notes	Marks
01.1	Producer		1
01.2	Predator	Also accept consumer.	1
01.3	Decreased They starved to death due to lack of food		1 1
01.4	A		1
02.1	Trees in the forest are taller than the single tree. The single tree has leaves at more levels than the trees in the forest (where the leaves are just near the top of the trees).		1 1
02.2	**Any two from:** Sunlight Water Mineral ions Space.		2
02.3	A square outline with a known size, e.g. 1 m × 1 m	Also accept: a device for counting the plants that appear within its area.	1
02.4	Three		1
02.5	Approximately 60%	Accept anything between 50% and 65%	1
02.6	It will decrease. Less light available for grass to grow. / The trees shade the ground.		1 1
02.7	She could collect more data both in the forest and near the single tree. More samples means more reliable results. She could take a transect from the single tree into the forest.		1 1 1 1
03.1	Bacterial		1
03.2	Less resistant bacteria are killed first / survival of the fittest. If course not completed, resistant bacteria survive. Resistant bacteria then reproduce.		1 1 1
03.3	Doctors only prescribe antibiotics for serious illnesses Restrict the agricultural use of antibiotics		1 1
04.1	A leaf		1
04.2	Evidence of the existence of organisms from hundreds of thousands of years ago.		1
04.3	The method of formation of other types of rock destroys the remains of the organisms.	Allow specific examples: e.g. the high temperature of igneous rocks destroys the remains.	1
04.4	How life has evolved How old animals and plants are	Accept any other reasonable answer.	1 1
05.1	Any figure in the range 12.9–15.1. Trend – darker colour to more mass loss. Darker colour – higher temperature / faster decay.		1 1 1
05.2	**Any two from:** Grass from same place Same mass of grass cuttings in each bag Same material for bag Same thickness of material for bag Same thickness / packing of material in the bag		2
06.1	D		1
06.2	B		1
06.3	It is found in the brain and responds to body conditions by secreting several hormones into the blood which the act on other glands which stimulate the release of other hormones.		1 1 1
07.1	Female reaction time better than male / females have faster reaction time than males.		1

<table>
<tr><th>Question Number</th><th>Answer</th><th>Notes</th><th>Marks</th></tr>
<tr><td>07.2</td><td>$\frac{0.31 + 0.32 + 0.29 + 0.32}{4}$
Answer is 0.31</td><td></td><td>1
1</td></tr>
<tr><td>07.3</td><td>Rapid / fast
Automatic / done without thinking</td><td></td><td>1
1</td></tr>
<tr><td>07.4</td><td>Impulse causes release of chemical / neurotransmitter from ends of sensory neurone.
Chemical / neurotransmitter diffuses across gap.
Chemical / neurotransmitter binds to receptor molecules on next / relay neurone.
This triggers electrical impulse in next / relay neurone.</td><td></td><td>1
1
1
1</td></tr>
<tr><td>08.1</td><td>39</td><td></td><td>1</td></tr>
<tr><td>08.2</td><td>Mitosis
Any two from:
Chromosomes are copied.
Two full sets of chromosomes are made.
Each set moves to the opposite end of the cell.
Any one from:
Cell divides in two.
Each new cell contains a complete set.</td><td></td><td>1
2
1</td></tr>
<tr><td>09.1</td><td>When humans breed plants / animals for particular genetic characteristics</td><td></td><td>1</td></tr>
<tr><td>09.2</td><td>Allele</td><td></td><td>1</td></tr>
<tr><td>09.3</td><td><table><tr><td></td><td>R</td><td>r</td></tr><tr><td>r</td><td>Rr</td><td>rr</td></tr><tr><td>r</td><td>Rr</td><td>rr</td></tr></table></td><td>2 marks if all are correct, 1 mark if only 1 is correct</td><td>2</td></tr>
<tr><td>09.4</td><td>One of the rr should be circled</td><td></td><td>1</td></tr>
<tr><td>09.5</td><td>50% or 1:1 or 1 in 2</td><td></td><td>1</td></tr>
<tr><td>09.6</td><td>Any three from:
Stabilises ecosystems
Preserves food chains
Preserves possible future crops
Preserves possible future medicines
Preserves interdependence of species</td><td></td><td>3</td></tr>
<tr><td>10.1</td><td>Indicative content
Control method 1
Pancreas monitors glucose level
Pancreas produces insulin if glucose level high
Glucose converted to glycogen
Glycogen stored in liver / cells
Control method 2
Pancreas produces glucagon if glucose level low
Glycogen converted to glucose by glucagon
Control method 3
Type 1: blood glucose levels tested regularly
Insulin injections if glucose level high
Control method 4
Type 2: diet control
Regular exercise</td><td>Level 3:
Correct descriptions of all four control methods.
Level 2:
Correct description of control method 1 and one other control method (2, 3 or 4).
Level 1:
One correct description of any control method.
Level 0:
No relevant content
Allow 3 marks for a full description of methods 3 and 4 only.</td><td>5–6
3–4
1–2
0</td></tr>
<tr><td>10.2</td><td>Any two from:
They:
filter the blood
remove water from the blood
remove ions from the blood
reabsorb glucose into the blood
reabsorb water into the blood
reabsorb ions into the blood.</td><td></td><td>2</td></tr>
</table>

Chemistry Paper 3 Foundation

Question Number	Answer	Notes	Marks
01.1	A mixture of metals		1
01.2	Brass – saxophone Bronze – statue	Also accept: Brass – statue Bronze – water pipe	1 1
01.3	**Any two from:** Steel is harder than iron. Steel is stronger than iron. Steel is less likely to corrode / rust than iron.	The answer must be a comparison.	2
02.1	Each row begins with elements with one outer electron.		1
02.2	Their boiling points increase as you go down the group.		1
02.3	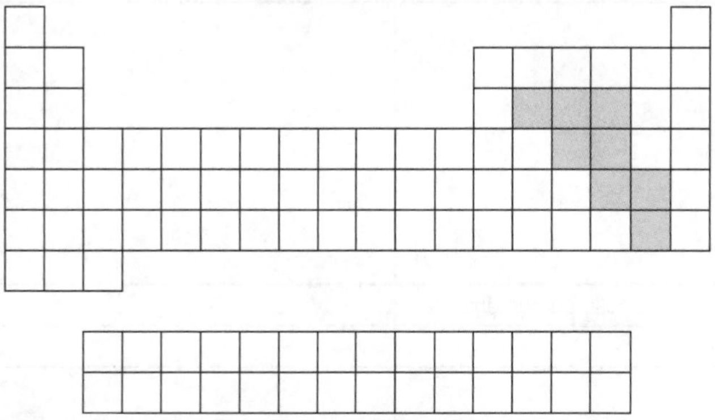	Give 1 mark for an X anywhere in the grey area.	1
02.4	They make an alkali when reacted with water.		1
02.5	The outer electron in sodium is further from the nucleus. Less energy needed to remove the outer electron / the outer electron is less tightly held / less attractive force from nucleus to outer electron.		1 1
03.1	Sulfuric acid and copper sulfate are solutions / aqueous. Copper oxide is a solid. Water is a liquid.	1 mark for each Award 2 marks for: They are solutions, It is a solid, It is a liquid.	2 1 1
03.2	Neutralisation		1
03.3	**Any two from:** • wear safety glasses • when not heating, have the bunsen burner on a yellow flame • make sure there is a clear space around the practical • take care when handling hot equipment • do not overheat the solution.		2
03.4	H^+		1
03.5	The pH started low and increased to 7.		1
04.1	High melting point and slippery		1
04.2	**Any two from:** high (tensile) strength high electrical conductivity high thermal conductivity.		2
04.3	High melting point because of: giant structure / lots of bonds / macromolecule strong bonds / lots of energy to break bonds. Does not conduct electricity because: there are no free / mobile electrons **or** all its electrons are used in bonding.		1 1 1
05.1	It has the same number of electrons and protons.		1
05.2	Number of protons in the ion: **26** Number of neutrons in the ion: **30** Number of electrons in the ion: **24**	Only award 1 mark if all three numbers are correct.	1

Question Number	Answer	Notes	Marks
05.3	**Protons:** the atomic number / number on the bottom left of symbol **Neutrons:** 56 – 26 = 30 / mass number – atomic number **Electrons:** 26 – 2 = 24 / atomic number but 2 electrons have been removed to make 2+		1 1 1
05.4	Magnesium loses electrons and oxygen gains electrons. Two electrons are transferred.		1 1
05.5	The magnesium ion has a charge of 2+. The oxide ion has a charge of 2–.		1 1
06.1	Carbon dioxide gas		1
06.2	Endothermic		1
06.3	All the iron nitrate must be used up.		1
06.4	Correct order: calcium, magnesium, zinc, copper. Order worked out using data in Table 2. More reactive metals show a greater rise in temperature.		1 1 1
06.5	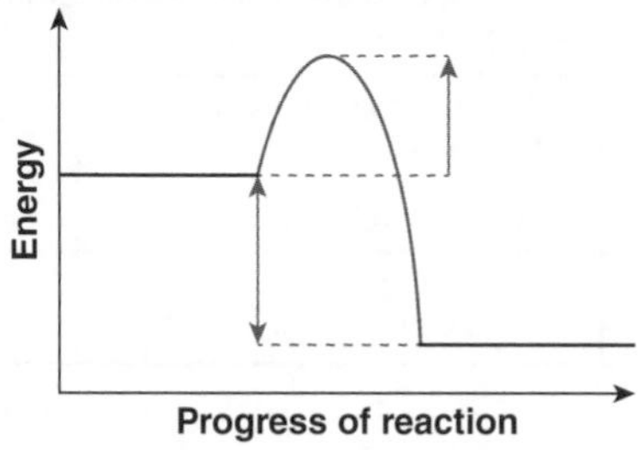 Activation energy: B Products: D Reactants: A Energy given out during the reaction: C	Award 3 marks if all answers are correct, 2 marks if one answer is wrong and 1 mark if one answer is correct.	3
07.1	Five		1
07.2	64 + 12 + (3 × 16) = 64 + 12 + 48 = 124	Award 1 mark for working, 1 mark for correct answer.	2
07.3	copper(II) carbonate ⟶ copper(II) oxide + carbon dioxide	Accept copper carbonate and copper oxide without (II)	1
07.4	12.35 – 7.95 = 4.40 (g)	Accept 4.4 (g)	1 1
08.1	The breakdown / decomposition of a substance using an electric current.	Also accept: using electricity.	1 1
08.2	The ions are not free to move		1
08.3	Anode: oxygen Cathode: copper		1 1
08.4	**Indicative content** • Molten sodium chloride – Sodium forms at the cathode; chlorine forms at the anode • Sodium chloride solution – Hydrogen gas forms at the cathode; chlorine at the anode • Molten sodium chloride only contains Na^+ and Cl^- ions • So when no competition and both ions are discharged • Sodium chloride solution contains Na^+; H^+, Cl^-, OH^- ions • H^+ is discharged in preference to Na^+ ions; Cl^- ions discharged in preference to OH^- ions	**Level 3** A fully detailed comparison of the two types of electrolysis **Level 2** A comparison of the two types of electrolysis, allowing some errors **Level 1** A brief comparison of the two types of electrolysis **Level 0** – No relevant content	5–6 3–4 1–2 0

Question Number	Answer	Notes	Marks
09.1	First test – the iodide converted (oxidised) to iodine. Bromine is more reactive than iodine. No reaction in second test because bromine is less reactive than chlorine.		1 1 1 1
09.2	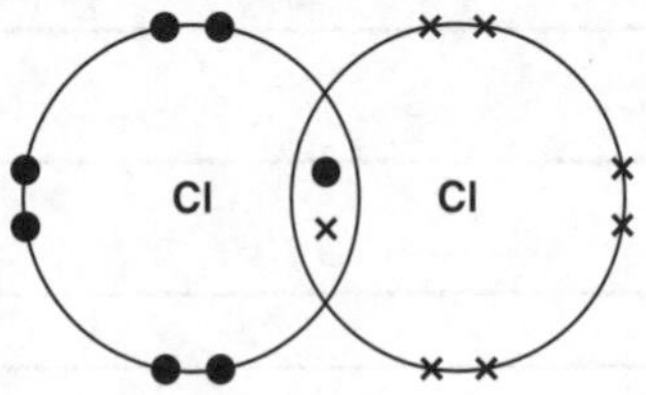 **or** 	Give 1 mark for the shared pair of electrons. Give 1 mark if the rest of the diagram is correct.	1 1
09.3	Chlorine has weaker forces between molecules / weaker intermolecular forces. Less energy is needed to separate molecules in chlorine.	Allow 'stronger' forces for iodine. Allow 'more energy' for iodine.	1 1
09.4	It has no free electrons / the electrons cannot move / all outer electrons are involved in bonding.		1

Chemistry Paper 4 Foundation

Question Number	Answer	Notes	Marks
01.1	Chlorine		1
01.2	Carbon dioxide		1
01.3	C and D		2
01.4	**Any two from:** • carbon monoxide joins with haemoglobin in the blood, • reducing its capacity to carry oxygen • person becomes very sleepy • eventually dies if not treated		2
01.5	Sulfur dioxide		1
01.6	**Any two from:** • damages plants • damages buildings • kills fish and other aquatic life.		2
02.1	Wood		1
02.2	Manufacturing the jeans and packaging		1
02.3	Meeting the needs of the people today without compromising the needs of future generations		1
02.4	Timber could be sustainable if forests are managed properly Timber is a renewable resource/could plant more trees		1 1
03.1	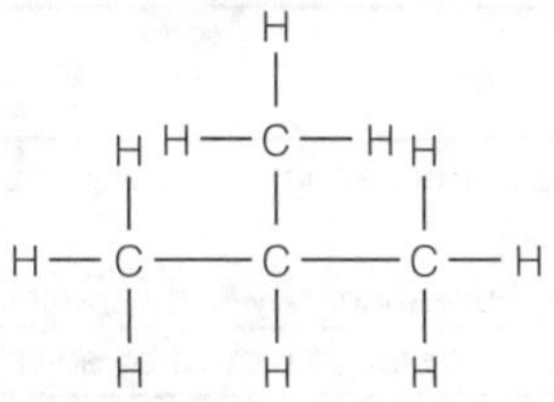		1
03.2	**Any two from:** Petrol Diesel Engine oil Tar Aviation fuel LPG Natural gas		2
03.3	A molecule containing carbon and hydrogen only		1 1
03.4	Evaporation and condensation	Award 1 mark for each correct answer	2
03.5	$CH_4 + 2O_2 \rightarrow CO_2 + 2H_2O$	Award 1 mark for inserting the correct formulae and 1 mark for the correct balancing.	2
03.6	They are oxidised.		1
04.1	**Any one from:** They act as a catalyst. They speed up the reaction. They provide a surface on which the reaction happens.		1
04.2	Breaking up / decomposing (large molecules) into smaller / more useful substances / molecules.		1 1
04.3	$C_{16}H_{34} \rightarrow C_{10}H_{22} + 3C_2H_4$	If balancing is not correct, allow 1 mark for: $C_{16}H_{34} \rightarrow C_{10}H_{22} + C_2H_4$	2
05.1	Dylan		1
05.2	The acid was the limiting reagent in her experiment / all of the acid had been used up in her experiment. Magnesium was the limiting reagent in the other experiments / all of the magnesium was used up in the other experiments.	Allow: magnesium in excess. Allow: acid in excess.	1 1

Question Number	Answer	Notes	Marks
05.3	mean rate = $\frac{\text{quantity of product formed}}{\text{time taken}} = \frac{94.5}{225} =$ 0.42 Unit = cm^3/s		1 1 1
05.4	The volume of gas will double because the volume of gas is dependent on the amount of magnesium.		1 1
06.1	**Indicative content** • Draw a line in pencil across the chromatography paper – approximately 2 cm up from the bottom. • Label each ink in pencil under the line. • At regular intervals along the pencil line, add a drop of each ink. Use the hairdryer to dry the ink. • Pour the solvent into the chromatography tank. • Use the hook to hang the paper in the tank, so that the pencil line is above the solvent. • Put on the lid. When the solvent line nearly reaches the top, remove the paper from the tank and leave to dry.	**Level 3:** Clear description of a method, in the correct sequence, that would produce a good chromatogram. A description of why some of the steps are taken. **Level 2:** A description of a method that uses the listed equipment. The steps taken are in the correct order to produce a chromatogram. **Level 1:** A basic description of a simple method that uses some of the listed equipment. **Level 0:** No relevant content	5–6 3–4 1–2 0
06.2	C and D		1
06.3	Ink D It has moved furthest up the paper.		1 1
06.4	The ratio of the distance moved by a compound to the distance moved by the solvent	Allow the correct equation for working out the R_f value: R_f value = $\frac{\text{distance moved by substance}}{\text{distance moved by solvent}}$	1
06.5	$0.86 = \frac{\text{distance moved by B}}{7.91} = 0.86 \times 7.91$ $= 6.8$	 6.80 / 6.802 / 6.8026 is worth 1 mark.	1 1
07.1	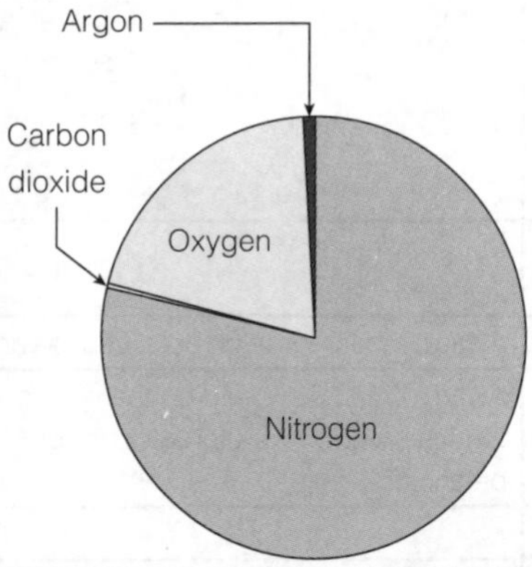		1
07.2	D, A, C, B	Allow 1 mark if D and A are in the correct order.	2
07.3	It is a simple or complex testable explanation put forward by scientists to try and explain observations/facts.		1 1
07.4	It cannot be proved because it was so long ago / there is insufficient evidence to confirm the theory.		1

Question Number	Answer	Notes	Marks
08.1	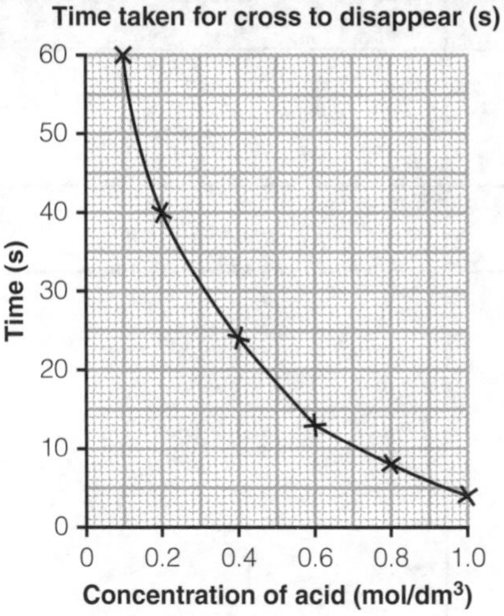 All six points correctly plotted Smooth curve	Allow 1 mark for four or five points correctly plotted; 1 mark deducted if the graph is plotted dot to dot rather than as a smooth curve.	2 1
08.2	Rate increases as concentration increases. Increased concentration means more crowded particles / more particles in same space / volume. More chance of collision / more frequent collisions.		1 1 1
08.3	The reaction times would be smaller / shorter / less.		1
09.1	Exothermic		1
09.2	It is reversible.		1
09.3	Add water		1
10.1	B Powder reacts faster / line steeper on graph because powder has a larger surface area. More chance of successful collisions / more frequent successful collisions.		1 1 1 1
10.2	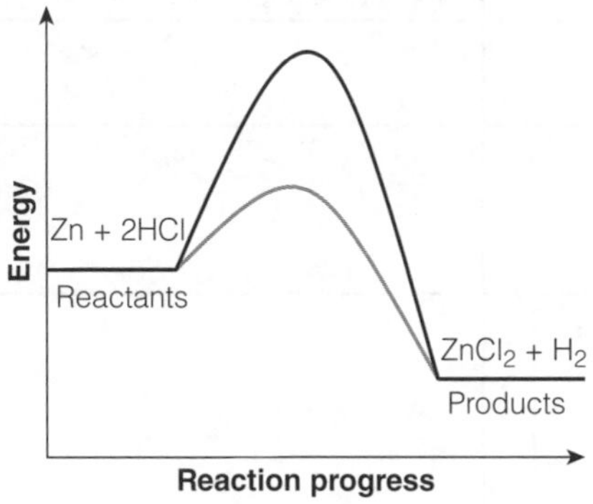	The curve must start at reactants, be lower than the original curve and end at products.	1

Physics Paper 5 Foundation

<table>
<tr><th>Question Number</th><th>Answer</th><th>Notes</th><th>Marks</th></tr>
<tr><td>01.1</td><td>Y lights up.
X and Y are both off.
X and Y are both on.</td><td></td><td>1
1
1</td></tr>
<tr><td>01.2</td><td>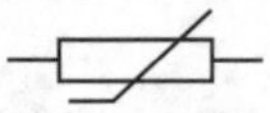</td><td></td><td>1</td></tr>
<tr><td>01.3</td><td>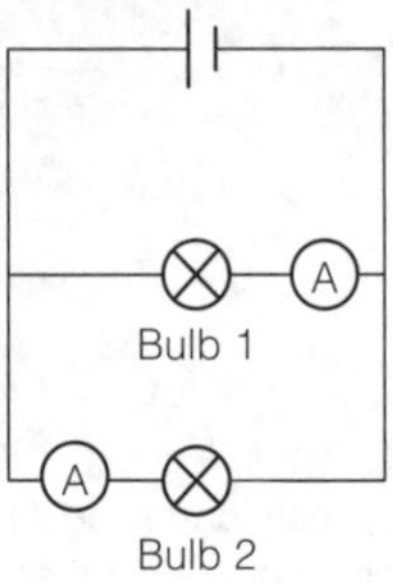
</td><td></td><td>1</td></tr>
<tr><td>01.4</td><td>$V = I \times R = 0.005 \times 1200$
$= 6\ V$
$\frac{6\ V}{1.5\ V}$ = 4 batteries needed</td><td></td><td>1
1
1</td></tr>
<tr><td>01.5</td><td>Diode
A diode only allows current to flow through in one direction.

So, with a positive potential difference, current flows but there is no current flowing if the potential difference is reversed.</td><td></td><td>1
1

1</td></tr>
<tr><td>02.1</td><td><table>
<tr><td>Isotope</td><td>Number of protons</td><td>Number of neutrons</td><td>Number of electrons</td></tr>
<tr><td>Carbon-12</td><td>6</td><td>6</td><td>6</td></tr>
<tr><td>Carbon-13</td><td>6</td><td>7</td><td>6</td></tr>
<tr><td>Carbon-14</td><td>6</td><td>8</td><td>6</td></tr>
</table></td><td>1 mark for each correct column</td><td>3</td></tr>
<tr><td>02.2</td><td>A neutron changes into a proton
by emitting a (high speed) electron.</td><td></td><td>1
1</td></tr>
<tr><td>02.3</td><td>The time taken for the activity / count rate to halve
or
the time taken for the number of nuclei of the isotope to halve.</td><td></td><td>1</td></tr>
<tr><td>02.4</td><td><table>
<tr><th>Number of half-lives</th><th>Time after death of organism in years</th><th>$^{14}C : ^{12}C$ ratio / 10^{-12}</th></tr>
<tr><td>0</td><td>0</td><td>1.000</td></tr>
<tr><td>1</td><td>5730</td><td>0.500</td></tr>
<tr><td>2</td><td>11 460</td><td>0.250</td></tr>
<tr><td>3</td><td>17 190</td><td>0.125</td></tr>
</table></td><td></td><td>1</td></tr>
<tr><td>02.5</td><td>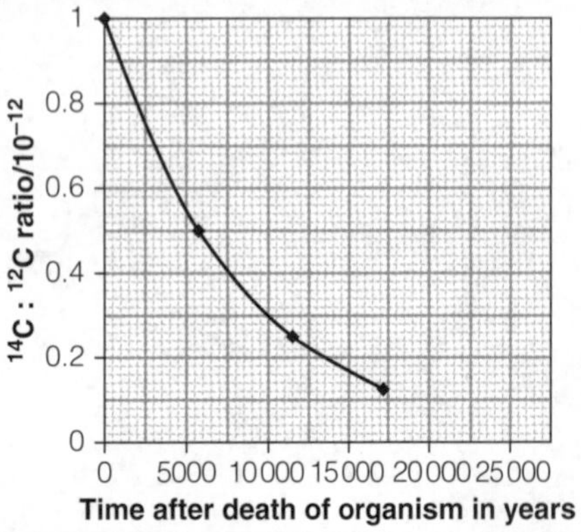
</td><td>Plotting points correctly
Smooth curve</td><td>1
1</td></tr>
<tr><td>02.6</td><td>10 000 (years)</td><td>Accept answers in the range 9500–10 500</td><td>1</td></tr>
</table>

<table>
<tr><th>Question Number</th><th>Answer</th><th>Notes</th><th>Marks</th></tr>
<tr><td>03.1</td><td>50 Hz, 230 V, ac</td><td></td><td>1</td></tr>
<tr><td>03.2</td><td>It does not need an earth wire.</td><td></td><td>1</td></tr>
<tr><td>03.3</td><td><table>
<tr><th>Wire</th><th>Name</th><th>Colour</th></tr>
<tr><td>A</td><td>Neutral</td><td>Blue</td></tr>
<tr><td>B</td><td>Live</td><td>Brown</td></tr>
<tr><td>C</td><td>Earth</td><td>Green and yellow stripes</td></tr>
</table></td><td>2 marks for all three answers correct,
1 mark for two correct answers</td><td>2</td></tr>
<tr><td>03.4</td><td>The earth wire stops the appliance becoming live.
It carries current if there is a fault.
It stops someone from being electrocuted if there is a fault.</td><td></td><td>1
1
1</td></tr>
<tr><td>04.1</td><td>Coal</td><td></td><td>1</td></tr>
<tr><td>04.2</td><td>Geothermal</td><td></td><td>1</td></tr>
<tr><td>04.3</td><td>Any one from:
• causes air pollution
• emits greenhouse gases
• mines spoil the countryside
Accept any other reasonable answer.</td><td></td><td>1</td></tr>
<tr><td>04.4</td><td>Economic/social reasons – it's cheaper to use fossil fuels.
Political reasons – lots of jobs will be lost if we stop using fossil fuels.</td><td></td><td>1
1</td></tr>
<tr><td>05.1</td><td>Position 4</td><td></td><td>1</td></tr>
<tr><td>05.2</td><td>Gravitational potential energy = mass × gravitational field strength × height or $E_p = mgh$
$E = 520 \times 10 \times 100 = 520\,000$ J or 520 kJ</td><td>1 mark for showing working, 1 mark for correct answer and units</td><td>1
2</td></tr>
<tr><td>05.3</td><td>Maximum gravitational potential energy at position 1.
Changes to kinetic energy in Positions 2–4 (as the cars go down the hill).</td><td></td><td>1
1</td></tr>
<tr><td>06.1</td><td>Indicative content
• Set up a bunsen burner, tripod and gauze.
• Half-fill the beaker with water, place it on the gauze and heat it using the bunsen burner.
• When the water is boiling, place one of the boiling tubes with the oil in the beaker and clamp it into place.
• Place the thermometer into the oil.
• When the temperature reaches 30°C, heat for a further 60 seconds using the stopwatch (accept other times).
• Record the new temperature. Repeat with the other oil.</td><td>Level 3:
A clear description of a method, in the correct sequence, that would produce valid results. A description of what is measured and at least one control variable.
Level 2:
A description of a method that uses the equipment. The steps taken are in the correct order to produce the desired result.
Level 1:
A basic description of a simple method that uses some of the equipment.
Level 0:
No relevant content
Accept variations on volume of water, temperature and time taken.</td><td>5–6
3–4
1–2
0</td></tr>
<tr><td>06.2</td><td>Wear safety goggles.
Take care when handling hot apparatus or do not heat oil directly</td><td></td><td>1
1</td></tr>
<tr><td>06.3</td><td>Olive oil
It has the lower specific heat capacity.
This means it takes less energy for it to heat up 1°C than the vegetable oil, which has a higher specific heat capacity.</td><td></td><td>1
1
1</td></tr>
<tr><td>07.1</td><td>Ice: regular arrangement – all particles touching
Water: irregular arrangement – particles touching
Water vapour: random arrangement – particles spaced</td><td>Accept correctly drawn particle diagrams.</td><td>1
1
1</td></tr>
<tr><td>07.2</td><td>The ice particles start to vibrate more
because the internal energy of the particles increases as thermal energy is transferred from the Sun.
Eventually, the particles have enough energy to move freely
in the liquid state.</td><td></td><td>1
1
1
1</td></tr>
<tr><td>07.3</td><td>Specific latent heat of fusion</td><td></td><td>1</td></tr>
</table>

Question Number	Answer	Notes	Marks
08.1	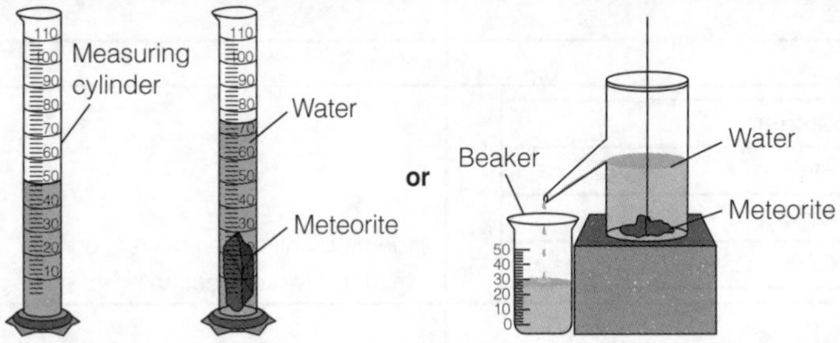	1 mark for drawing appropriate apparatus 1 mark for showing that water is displaced The diagram must have labels to gain full marks	1 1
08.2	**Any two from:** reduces random experimental error can calculate a mean value can identify anomalous results.		2
08.3	Mass	Accept weight	1
08.4	Nickel		1
09.1	Lead		1
09.2	energy = power × time $= 100 \times 85$ $= 8500\text{ J}$		 1 1
09.3	$\text{temperature change} = \dfrac{\text{change in thermal energy}}{\text{mass} \times \text{specific heat capacity}}$ $= \dfrac{9065}{0.5 \times 490}$ $= 37°\text{C}$ final temperature = 22 + 37 = 59°C		1 1 1

Physics Paper 6 Foundation

Question Number	Answer	Notes	Marks
01.1	2.5 N		1
01.2	0.1 N		1
01.3	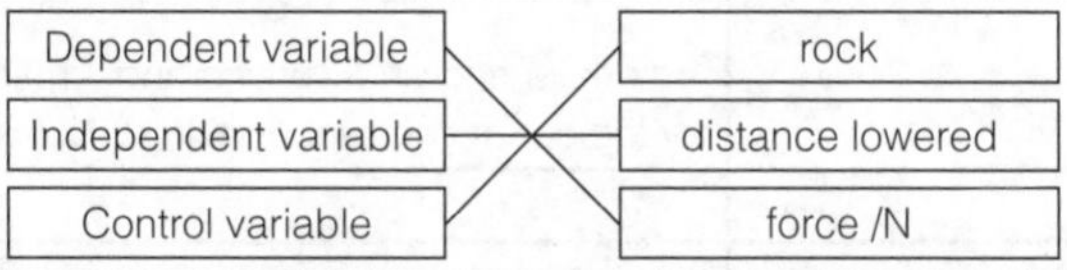		2
01.4	The reading decreases as the rock is lowered in the water No (further) change when the rock is fully submerged		1 1
01.5	Use a ruler/measure distance lowered Have suitable increments, e.g. measure force every 1 cm lowered		1 1
01.6	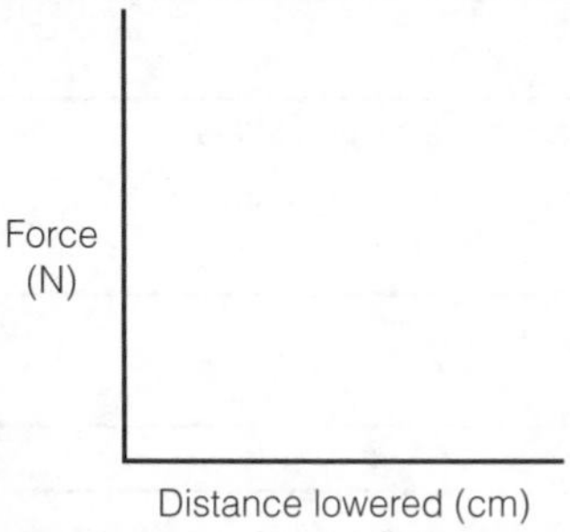		1
02.1	A and D		1
02.2	Force X increases		1
02.3	weight = mass × gravitational field = 55 × 10 = 550 N		1
02.4	Force X = 550 N The forces balance each other / the forces reach an equilibrium / force X = force Y	Accept weight for force Y Accept air resistance for force X	1 1
02.5	4 and 5		1
03.1	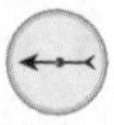		1
03.2	They point to the North pole because the Earth has a magnetic field	For 2 marks, accept: the needles align to the Earth's magnetic field	1 1
03.3	They will move to point in a circle.		1 1
03.4	Iron and steel	1 mark for each correct answer.	2
03.5	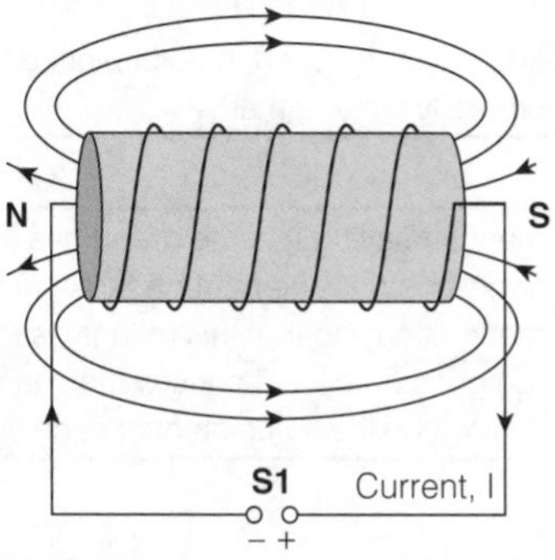	Magnetic field should represent that of a normal bar magnet. It must include direction of field from N to S. Uniform lines should be drawn through the wire and around the top and bottom.	1 1 1
03.6	Increase current Increase the number of coils		1 1
03.7	**Any two from:** • electric doorbells • cranes used in scrapyards to move vehicles • door locks • relay switches in computers. Accept any other reasonable answers.		2
04.1	C		1
04.2	D		1

Question Number	Answer	Notes	Marks
04.3	Infrared		1
04.4	frequency = $\frac{\text{wave speed}}{\text{wavelength}}$		1
04.5	frequency = $\frac{\text{wave speed}}{\text{wavelength}} = \frac{3 \times 10^8}{0.12}$ $= 2.5 \times 10^9$ Hz	1 mark for showing working and 1 mark for the correct answer and unit	2
05.1	10 m/s		1
05.2	acceleration = $\frac{\text{change of velocity}}{\text{time taken}}$ $= \frac{15 - 0}{3}$ = 5 = 5m / s^2		1 1 1
05.3	distance 0–3s = 0.5 × 15 × 3 = 22.5 m distance 3–6s = 15 × 3 = 45 m total distance = 22.5 + 45 = 67.5 m	distance = area under line distance = velocity × time	1 1 1
05.4	Slowing down / decelerating / negative acceleration at a uniform / constant rate.		1 1
06.1	10 mm (62 – 52)		1
06.2	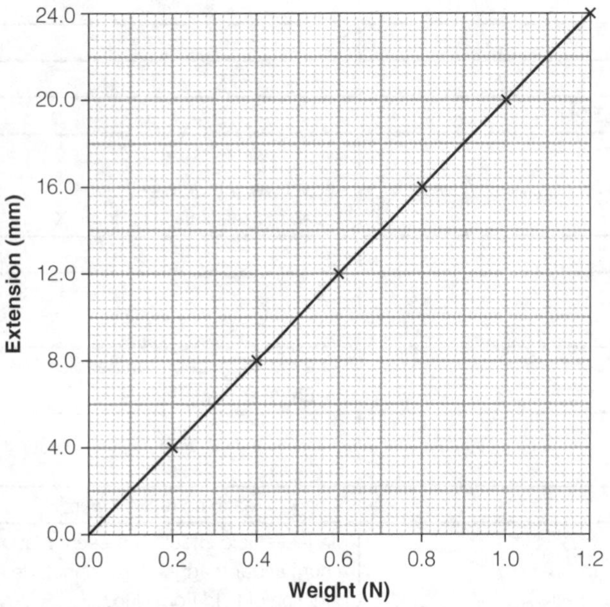	All points correctly plotted Single straight line passing through the origin Deduct 1 mark for each point plotted incorrectly, up to 2 marks.	2 1
06.3	0.7 N		1
06.4	The extension of the spring is directly proportional to the weight stretching the spring.	1 mark for saying that the graph has a straight line passing through the origin. 1 mark for saying that this means as the force goes up by 1, it causes the spring to stretch by the same amount each time.	2
06.5	Repeat the experiment. Calculate the mean results.		1 1
07.1	It could influence the result.		1
07.2	You can take a direct reading without doing any calculations.		1
07.3	The shorter the distance the ruler drops, the faster the reaction time.		1
07.4	$\frac{(15.0 + 16.0 + 14.0)}{3} = 15.0$	1 mark for showing working, 1 mark for correct answer	2
07.5	Trial 2, Kassim, 20.0 cm Perhaps Kassim was not ready or lost concentration.		1 1
07.6	Kassim has a faster reaction time than Farah.		1

Question Number	Answer	Notes	Marks
07.7	Kassim. He has a faster reaction time than Farah. So when the starting gun sounds, he has more thinking time to respond.		1 1 1
08.1	**Indicative content** Include the equation: stopping distance = thinking distance + braking distance **(Increased) speed** Increases thinking distance Same thinking time but greater distance travelled Increases braking distance More kinetic energy to be absorbed by the brakes Stopping distance increases	**Level 3:** Use stopping distance equation to give a correct detailed explanation of how all three conditions affect the stopping distance, and one reference to adjusting driving to suit conditions. **Level 2:** Use stopping distance equation to give a correct detailed explanation of how two out of the three conditions affect the stopping distance. **Level 1:** Use stopping distance equation to give a correct detailed explanation of how one condition affects the stopping distance. **Level 0:** No relevant content	5–6 3–4 1–2 0
	Road conditions Anything on the road surface will increase braking distance. The surface will be slippery / less friction / less grip. No effect on thinking distance Stopping distance increases	Examples: water, snow, ice, leaves, mud Do not accept poor weather / poor visibility / fog	
	Alcohol Increases thinking distance Increases reaction time No effect on braking distance Stopping distance increases Idea that slower speeds reduce chance of accident or that adjusting speed to suit conditions reduces chance of accident.		

Notes

Notes

Notes